T0336327

THE *Flourishing* COMMUNITY

A Story of **HOPE** FOR
AMERICA'S DISTRESSED PLACES

Brad Ketch

Forefront
BOOKS

Published by Forefront Books.

Library of Congress Control Number: 2022914873

Print ISBN: 978-1-63763-160-7
E-book ISBN: 978-1-63763-161-4

Cover Design by Bruce Gore, Gore Studio, Inc.
Interior Design by Bill Kersey, KerseyGraphics

Contents

Contents 3

Glossary 5

Foreword by Paul Young 9

Introduction: A Knock at the Door 17

I Find My Own Calcutta 23

Proximity 37

Poverty, Inc. 51

Things Get Real 67

We Begin the Conversation 87

Let a Hundred Flowers Bloom 105

The Black Chapter 123

Place Matters 139

Let's Part Friends 157

The Dam Breaks 181

Together 189

Epilogue: A Knock at the Door 203

Go FISH! 207

Under the Hood: Notes on How We Set
    and Run the Businesses 227

Resources for Learning More 235

Acknowledgments 237

Notes 239

Glossary

Aid: When a government unit or a major philanthropy gives cash or goods to another country or to an on-the-ground agency in order to accomplish a specific purpose.

Asset Based Community Development (ABCD): Building on what is already working in a community.

Betterment: People growing their own capacity for improvement at their pace, and at their direction, using resources that others make available.

Capacity Building: The capacity to act is built when the local community participates in their growth, when leaders emerge, when individuals have more skills, when there is a shared understanding of the problems that the community faces, when there is a shared vision for the future, when there is a widely understood agenda, when there is tangible progress toward goals, and when effective organizations and institutions can guard the process for the long term.

Capital: Another word for asset, or something that has value that can be spent.

Community: In this book, a set of relationships that are bounded by geography. A more common definition is a set of relationships that are bounded by identity.

Development: Those programs that address the bigger picture: the systems of health care, of government, of schools, of faith communities, of infrastructure and other categories that encourage people's abilities to naturally rise (or hold them down).

FISH: Financial, Informational, Social, and Human assets.

Holistic: Putting all aspects of society to work on the common goal—the businesses, the government, the health systems, the schools, the faith centers, the media, and our neighbors. The results are holistic too: better health, higher income, less violence, greater educational attainment, healthier families, and so on. Holistic thinking means that each of these elements cannot be understood as a standalone thing. Each must be understood in its relation to the whole. If you're not doing it all, then you're not doing it at all.

Human Flourishing: In the context of community development, achieving shalom.

Income Inequality: The extent to which incomes are unevenly distributed in a society. The more equal a given country is, the greater the social cohesion, the lower the crime rate, the better the health outcomes, and the faster the economic growth.

Proximity: Reducing my distance to the poor from miles to the width of a café table. And staying there for as long as it takes until I am more interested in the real you than I am in the idea of you.

Poverty: The result of broken relationships between individuals and their context.

Poveteers: People who make their living off of the deficiencies in a community. They study the needs, nurture funding, and create institutions that are dependent upon the existence of these deficiencies. The poor are not the primary beneficiaries of Poverty, Inc. They are the raw materials. The beneficiaries are the people who make a living from Poverty, Inc., and the investors who are earning a return.

Relief: Those programs that spend aid dollars on specific felt and immediate needs.

Shalom: Peace along five dimensions—self, family, community, God, and the environment.

Social Capital: The network of relationships, norms, and resources that sets the stage for human flourishing. People who are high in social capital flourish more than people who are low in it.

System: A combination of public and private sectors defined through policy, power, and personal positions that instills a defined network of structures and hierarchies that get to dictate three very important factors:

1. Who is normal?
2. What is normal?
3. How is normalcy achieved?

Foreword by Paul Young

*B*rad Ketch and I have known each other for over fifteen years. There are those rare friendships that don't require work and easily pick up where they left off, regardless of the time that has passed. Such relationships aren't embedded with hidden expectations. Ours is one of those and is certainly a gift to me.

In these pages you will come to know the CDC, an astounding community of people who represent as diverse a group as I have ever encountered and who have challenged by their very efforts and successes the entrenched and often blindly accepted doctrines of community development. My personal involvement with the CDC has been as an engaged participant waving and cheering from the cheap seats. I have watched its struggles, and now the dramatic and unpredictable triumphs, resulting from embracing the risk involved in trusting what resides in human beings, especially those considered poor and marginal. This story is counterintuitive to current and often patriarchal social agendas. It is important because it is unexpected and myste-rious, as must be anything fundamentally relational. You will meet real people who will surprise you and challenge you, and other precious folk who are enmeshed in the "way it has always been done," or others to whom fear-motivated power matters more than person.

I cannot adequately express to you how important this work and book are and how deeply surprising and emotionally connecting you will discover it to be. To be invited to write this foreword is an honor unlike any other.

So, to enter into *The Flourishing Community* I would like to employ the way of a parable. The story below did not happen, but that does not mean that it isn't true...

———

"Okay, bring him in," said the important Man sitting at his orga-nized desk in his carefully adorned office. He rose as Brad entered the room.

"Mr. Ketch?" he asked as he stretched out his hand in greeting.

The visitor shook his hand. "Brad would be fine."

"Brad then it is. Please have a seat," said the Man pointing to one of the chairs in front of his desk. He sat down and shuffled through some of the papers.

"I've been looking at your résumé and work history," said the Man without looking up. "Quite impressive. Undergrad in Economics, master's in management...from Kellogg Grad School, no less, extensive and successful experience in sales, you founded a couple companies, CEO of a semiconductor company...publicly traded, no less. Both hard skills and soft expertise and then your time with Community Development of Oregon, and even some international experience in the Philippines." He picked up the pages of the résumé and organized them into a neat pile on his desk before looking up.

"Very impressive, Ben, very impressive."

"Brad."

The Man raised his eyebrows before looking down at the pages and then back up, smiling.

"Of course it is. Your résumé is extensive and remarkable, exactly the kind of talent that we like to attract to our real estate development company." The Man leaned in a little. "That is why you are here, is it not? To get the lay of the land, to see what possibilities lay in front of you?"

"Well, I … admit that I want to learn more. I'm looking for clarity."

"Excellent!" exclaimed the Man. "Clarity is essential when you are facing the future and making decisions that will affect you in the long term. You are aware of our project, I assume?"

"In a general sense."

Ben, I think you will love it. The area we are working to secure is a blight, housed by people who are existing on the bottom rungs of society. Those people have nowhere else to go. Most of them are refugees from other countries. Many of those poor people don't even speak English. They can't even read their own language, for God's sake. There are gang problems in that area, drugs and who knows what else, and we mean to clean it up, transform it into retail and multifamily housing. And," he looked quickly at the file, "your skill set seems ideal to help implement such a plan."

"And what exactly are you going to do with *'those people'*?" Brad asked.

"What people?"

"The ones you mentioned in the blight list. Those poor refugees who don't speak English."

"Help them, of course. It's not like we don't care. We will get some tutors to help them speak English, get them job training, help them transition into the American way, maybe help them find housing somewhere better—you know, that sort of thing. Look, they would be happier somewhere else. Our goal is to save the larger community, make it stronger and more viable, and of course, do it at a profit. Takes real smarts," he pointed to his head. "And critical...uh, what's the term...?"

"Critical-thinking skills?"

"That's it, Ben! It takes critical-thinking skills to navigate the politics and local cultural issues to work it out. But we already have the support of local authorities and politicians. Everyone wants this area cleaned up and economically productive."

"You have the support of '*those people*' too?"

"What people?"

"'*Those people*', our neighbors who are immigrants, refugees, and low income?"

"They don't have enough skill or knowledge to make a true decision for themselves. They are not motivated, and we mean to change that. Don't you see, all of this is for *their* benefit. We will give them a hand up, a step to a better life, while solving real world issues and making all of this a win-win outcome." He sat back.

"Well, how exactly are you going to ..." Brad hesitated and that was all the Man needed.

"Bob, we can get to the nuts and bolts of all this once you are signed on, but for now why don't we talk in general terms. You're a communicator. You know the power of words, of language, to help steer conversation toward a desired outcome. There are a lot of people out there who don't want change and a bunch who want change, but in the wrong way. So, language is key to maintaining our goals and objectives while convincing the community and the politicians that our way is best for everyone."

Brad sat silent.

"Let me give you a couple of examples." The Man leaned forward, obviously energized by the conversation, even though largely one-sided.

"Listen to this. This is a good example. We don't waste valuable time, especially if we can help someone. Did you get that? Never hurts to have a bit of social self-consciousness that we can mix into a statement. People, especially young people, eat that sort of thing up."

Brad remained silent.

"Here is another one that you will need in this work." He made a grand gesture with his arms. "We tried that and it didn't work."

"Have you tried it?" Brad interjected.

"Tried what?" The Man looked a little confused.

"You said, 'We tried that, and it didn't work.' Did you try it?"

"Oh!" the man thought for a second before responding, "It doesn't matter whether we actually tried whatever 'it' is. I'm sure that someone tried it, somewhere. It matters that we don't want to waste any…."

"…of your valuable time," Brad finished the sentence.

"Exactly, Ben!" the man stated triumphantly and sat back in his chair smiling. Then he leaned forward again and lowered his voice. "Time is valuable. Time is money, and whatever 'it' is, will only be a waste of time."

"But…what if it helps people?"

"Then it is just a bonus. Oh, listen, here's another gem." He broadened his arms again and stated, "We are here for the long haul. Sometimes it means that if we aren't able to help the few, and we surely will try, it is only because it is more important to help the many."

Silence hung in the air as if holy, a silence that Brad broke. "Would the 'few' investors count?"

"Absolutely! The investors always count. It is because of them that we can help the many." The Man didn't even take a breath. "Oh, how about this one?" he said enthusiastically. "We already have a system for that, created by very smart people who studied all this for years. Our way is the best and has proven itself over time."

"Has it?"

"Ben, just look at our track record. Once you have succeeded with something, why change it? If it ain't broke, don't fix it. Everybody knows that." He paused, almost for theatrical emphasis. "So, Ben, what do you think?"

Brad waited a moment, thinking. "Are you familiar with the Hebrew writings?"

The Man looked surprised. "Hebrew writings? Not that I am aware of."

"Well, there is a story about a young boy, mid-teens maybe, the youngest of a large family. He was given the worst job in the family business, taking care of sheep out in the scrublands. It was out there that he learned to use a sling, a weapon that had enough power that he was able to kill a bear and a desert lion who threatened his sheep."

"Impressive," stated the Man, not sure where the conversation had gone.

"Word came that his older brothers had joined the military, so he went out to the battlefield to see them. Their army was on one side of the valley and the other army on the other side. Seems that the other guys had a secret weapon, a giant of a man estimated to be somewhere between seven feet to ten feet tall."

"Even more impressive," stated the Man, now mildly curious but wondering what this had to do with anything.

"The agreement between the armies was that two warriors would fight to the death and whoever won, so did their army and nation. Nobody wanted to fight the giant. He was huge, dressed in bronze armor that shone in the sun, and he carried a massive spear and huge sword. The shepherd boy's king offered fame and reward to anyone who would go out onto the battlefield and fight the guy, but everyone was too afraid.

"The boy was frustrated and offered his services to the king to fight the giant and, surprisingly, the king accepted—on one condition. The boy had to wear the king's armor. Out of respect and tradition, the boy tried on the armor, but it was too large and unwieldy, and he finally took it off. I can imagine the king talking to the boy, saying, 'It has always been done this way before, we have a track record to prove it.' But the boy insisted and walked out onto the battlefield with only a sling."

"The kid is going to be killed. I can see where this is going!" The Man was now more than curious.

"Maybe not. You see, there are some downsides to being a giant. It comes with a cost. This giant couldn't move very fast, especially with all the heavy armor. It turned out that he was more an image to instill terror into their opponents, a commercial for power. If you got close, he could kill you, but if you stayed at a distance, out of range of his weapons, it became clear what he was—a false and inflexible imitation of power. The giant couldn't respond to change, was unable to move quickly when faced with something new, and was terribly nearsighted. He called to the boy to come closer, within range of his traditional weapons, but the boy wasn't stuck in the 'way we have always done things.' With one sling and one stone, he knocked out the giant, took the huge man's own weapon, and cut off his head."

There was quiet in the room as the Man thought. Finally, he stated. "Wow, I have to say that in your story, I wanted to be the giant."

Brad hesitated, "You *are* the giant."

The Man looked bewildered, "So, does this mean that you don't want a job here? I am a bit confused."

"I got exactly what I came for—clarity. I am grateful to you for helping me with that. Thank you!"

Brad stood and held out his hand. "Well, I should be going. I wouldn't want to waste any more of your valuable time."

"Well, Bob," the Man rose to his feet. "I must say this has been an unusual meeting, but I appreciate you coming by. If things don't work out, you are welcome to come back here."

For those of you who read this foreword, you may be thinking it odd. It is a parable, of course, and such stories tend to be written through another lens. They are true but not *real. I invite you to revisit this parable when you have finished reading this brilliant and insightful book, which is both true* and *real.*

—Paul Young, author, *The Shack*

A Knock at the Door

When the doorbell rings at 5:30 in the morning, it is never good news. I live on a quiet country road just outside Portland, Oregon. All the houses are on five-acre plots, and I drop the word "estate" when describing them. When people learn where I live, they always say, "Oh, I know exactly which one you're talking about. I love that one!" There are two miles of fencing and metal gates that swing open only for us. Private, quiet, insulated.

A slight Latino teenager shuffles on the porch. I have a son about his age who is asleep upstairs. The kid looked down, and off to the left, and maybe at me, and says, "I need help."

I looked around and saw no cars. "How did you get here?"

"I was driving with my friends, and they stopped and pulled me out of the car, and they hit me on the head and took all of my stuff and threw me in your bushes. I don't have a phone anymore. Can you drive me home?"

"You got assaulted and robbed? Let's call the police!"

"No! I just need to get home, man. It's like three miles from here, over by Stark and 192nd. Can you help me?"

So, drugs, then. What the hell? Why was this happening right here, right now, and to me? I was supposed to go lift weights with my neighbor from down the street, who was supposed to be here any minute. I did not have time for this.

Then I think twice. "My friend and I are driving by that area anyway. Just wait on the porch, and we'll help you out."

Scott pulled up in his Mercedes right on cue. His facial expression told me he was silently appalled at the dirty teenager sliding into the back seat. "Can't he find another way home?" he said under his breath.

"We're driving right by his place," I said. "I mean, you can't not help him out."

On the brief trip to his apartment, I quizzed Renaldo about what had happened to him. I'll be honest—I had no frame of reference for this kid's life, and I did not understand what I was hearing. But I could process what I was seeing at his apartment: a car up on blocks, a Little Mermaid sheet in the living-room window where curtains ought to be, and a dirty, torn screen door. The parking lot abutted land that held a strip club, an hourly motel where people cooked meth, and the hub of the narcotics business. So that was how Renaldo connected to the drug culture.

He mumbled a *gracias* and we pulled out. As we did, a thought occurred to me—Renaldo could have been my kid. Despite how close they were to where I lived, I'd thought that I was insulated from him and his community. But he invaded my zen anyway.

I couldn't have known it then, but the memory of Renaldo would dog my steps as I encountered an ever-growing stream of Renaldos and fought hard to understand them and to work with them to create solutions. It became a ten-year quest that would end with me demolishing that strip club and meth house next to Renaldo's apartment and opening a new multi-million-dollar urban renewal project directly across the parking lot from where I dropped him that bewildering morning.

In the ten years since that knock at my door, the journey that Renaldo ignited would take me into glittering penthouse board-rooms, apartments used by sex-traffickers, tense confrontations with powerful politicians, and heartbreaking encounters with billionaires. I would visit those places and people in search of solutions—for the world's Renaldos and for me.

Working to lift up the poor was not a new concept to me. I have always given money to causes, and I have served on boards of directors for nonprofits. I enjoyed the "can-do" environment of most of them, and I had thought seriously about joining one full time once I was satisfied with the level of retirement savings I had set aside. In fact, when Renaldo knocked on my door, I was chair of a shelter for homeless families started by Cathe, a friend of mine. I was known around town because of my connection to this organization, and I was getting pretty good at raising money for it. But in truth, I was happy to be one step removed from the families that trudged through our doors every week. When Cathe would encourage me to get to know the families, I would say, "I do my compassion at the wholesale level, so that you and your staff can do compassion at the retail level."

Many people feel this way, don't they? Don't you? Aren't we all busy enough that personal involvement with people in need isn't really an option? Or at least that's how we feel. That's certainly where I was on the morning of Renaldo's knock. And yet—somewhere inside, I felt as if a different response might be required.

Later that night over a glass of Oregon pinot noir, I told my wife, Lynn, about my morning. Lynn is a far better human being than I am, and for reasons only she understands, loves me. Lynn was raised all over the US by a family serving in the Public Health Service. In childhood, she had been the only white girl among indigenous kids in remote Alaskan villages and Southwestern US reservations. If Lynn regards anyone in her life as *other*, it is probably people who are as white as she is. Always a step ahead of me, Lynn waits patiently for me to grow.

Until Renaldo knocked at my door, I liked my comfort circle. It had never occurred to me that this ever-shrinking circle was changing, becoming toxic to my culture—and even to me. Lynn knew that my privilege wasn't nearly as good for me as I thought.

"So, what do you want to do?" Lynn asked. "Drop the kid off and pretend that this never happened? Or might this call for a response from you?" Lynn had just completed her Certificate of Public Health from Oregon Health & Science University, and she knew a lot more than I did about who a kid like Renaldo is and *why* he was on my doorstep at 5:30 a.m., miles from home. That evening beside the fire, Lynn unfolded for me many of the themes we will be exploring in this book. She laid out for me the concept of the social determinants of health, the world of community development, how diversity is changing America, and the pathways forward that people are forging all over the US. What she was explaining was why poverty exists at the scale it does in America.

To me, some of this sounded so touchy-feely. I countered with the argument that for a community to thrive, it must have financial interventions on a huge scale. I explained that "the system"—mainly our government through our taxes—is supposed to take care of people like Renaldo. That people like Renaldo's parents must take personal responsibility. Not *my* responsibility. *Their* responsibility.

Lynn and I finally ran out of words and arguments and sat staring at each other, both realizing that neither of us saw the whole picture. For people to prosper, they must live in functioning communities. For communities to function, they must align both the hard elements—capital, public policy, land use, environment, taxes, and legal; and the soft elements—civic engagement, culture, faith communities, and equity—into one cohesive thing. It sank in for both of us that the solutions to poverty are complex, elusive, and radical.

Really too much to take on.

Above our pay grades.

So there.

But Renaldo would not settle. His persistently difficult life did not have to be this way. It was not the Fates that dictated that Renaldo would live a hopeless life—it was our culture. Lynn and I could think of dozens of changes, both large and small, that together could bring hope back into Renaldo's life.

She posed the question again: "So, what do you want to do?"

It was funny that her question, and Renaldo's invasion, came at the time that they did. I was already at a crossroads, both personally and professionally. After

So, what do you want to do?

the market crash of 2008, the strategies that had worked so well for me for so long had stopped working. The semiconductor company I had founded and owned, and of which I was CEO, went broke. I had stopped working, and I was out of money.

I was gearing up, mid-career, for a complete life change, and I was open to working full time in a different field. Maybe now the time had come to work for a nonprofit. But the problem was: If I was going to enter into poverty work, I wanted to enter it from a position of financial independence and power. If I entered it right now, after a year of not working at all and running down the savings account, I would enter it identifying with the poor. That seemed silly to me.

How could anyone who was poor himself tell people how to get out of poverty?

Now, I wouldn't have it any other way.

I could feel it coming over me, almost physically. I had spent years negotiating with my future and my calling. Time to stop negotiating and step up. I was ready to answer the knock at the door, even if it took me in directions that seemed radical.

"I'm not going back to tech, dear. And I don't know what else to do. Let's go where this road leads us."

"Maybe we should just do what Mother Teresa said."

"Mother Teresa? What does she have to do with this?"

"Well. People, especially rich people, came to her from all over the world to give her money or to volunteer. She turned them away. Here's what she said: 'Stay where you are. Find your own Calcutta. Find the sick, the suffering, and the lonely, right where you are—in your own homes and in your own families, in homes and in your workplaces and in your schools. You can find Calcutta all over the world, if you have eyes to see. Everywhere, wherever you go, you find people who are unwanted, unloved, uncared for, just rejected by society—completely forgotten, completely left alone.'"

You know what happened, starting that night?

I found my own Calcutta.

CHAPTER ONE

I Find My Own Calcutta

*K*iesel called out from the kitchen, "Coffee is on if you want it." Five years had gone by between Renaldo's interruption of my world and this mug of warmth—warmth that emanated from the man who brewed it. Kiesel is old and tall and thin, and he reminds people of Obi Wan Kenobi (the Alec Guinness version, not the Ewan McGregor one). He's a hippie who worked in Nigeria for years, training leaders to develop their communities and their faith. Over time, Kiesel's work has proven to be wildly successful, because he actually listened to emerging indigenous leaders, walked with them, and answered questions only when asked. He stubbornly insisted on a bottom-up approach instead of a top-down approach. Kiesel is my guide, my fellow wine enthusiast, my "desert father."

Kiesel and I talked for hours while the rain pounded on the windowpanes. What's great about Kiesel is that he notices the same things that I do. We were both intrigued that a very distressed neighborhood—Renaldo's world—existed just outside the boundary of one of America's richest cities, Portland. We saw how the rich and the poor are elbow to elbow, but living in different worlds, and how this disconnection was getting worse. It seemed to us that evidence of this disconnection was everywhere, mostly just below the surface, then sometimes popping up and pointing out its hold over our country. Kiesel and I admitted to each other that "disconnection" as a topic of discussion was big—so big it was hard to even think about.

But whether we liked it or not, "disconnection" was being dropped off on everyone's doorstep as surely as Renaldo had been dumped on mine. A few years later, the COVID pandemic would reveal to everyone the depth of our country's problem. "We're all in this storm together!" went the thought, until a tired single mom or frontliner would shoot back, "We may all be in the same storm, but we're not all in the same boat!" The disconnected people we used to ignore were now marching in the streets. And all of us who have means were being forced to decide: turn others away, or load them up in our car and drive them home.

Kiesel said, "Every American I know feels that they are living in momentous times. As a nation, we have been perched on the highest branch of the tree of nations during our lifetimes, our parents' lifetimes, and their parents' lifetimes. But lately our perch has become precarious. Many of us feel that we are falling off, and that once off, we will never get back on."

Kiesel's statement made me think about the stark disparities between the rich and the poor in developing countries.

When I was a technology executive, I hired a group of engineers in India. One day when I was visiting them, I was threading through traffic on a motorbike taxi and passed a Rolex dealership in a free-standing glass building with gold fixtures. But one of the outside walls was used by a farmer to prop up a tarp that formed his oxen stable. The shit-infused mud lent a new aura to the Rolex brand. How do the rich people of India accept these stark disparities? Don't they feel a twinge of conscience? Doesn't it cramp their consumerist high when they walk into that store? Don't they wonder if something should be done to reduce the inequality?

Income inequality is the extent to which incomes are unevenly distributed in a society. All things being equal, the more equal a given country is, the greater the social cohesion, the lower the crime rate, the better the health outcomes, and the faster the economic growth. And the worse that it is, the worse off everyone is—even the richest 1 percent.

Inequality is not a vague concept. It is a number measured by a tool called the Gini index, and every country in the world has a number on the index. India's number used to be awful, and America's used to be pretty good. But in the last twenty years, we have slumped into a Gini index that is the same as theirs. Today in Portland, where I live, Rolex and ox dung may not sit side by side, but homeless tents and million-dollar houses share the same block.

Could it really be true that Renaldo's neighborhood is now no different than Calcutta? I had to find out. If so, this was a truth that required action. If not, then I would not feel so troubled.

COULD ROCKWOOD AND CALCUTTA REALLY BE THE SAME?

The place that my friend and I dropped Renaldo off that morning is called Rockwood. I grew up around here, and people I know sneer at Rockwood. "The only good thing that comes out of Rockwood is the road!" my high-school friend said.

A place like Rockwood is a liminal place. You find liminal places when you go past the boundary of one place and before you arrive at another place. The eastern border of Portland is formed by 162nd Avenue, and Rockwood begins on 163rd—past the boundary. Gresham proper is down the road five miles, and historically had nothing to do with Rockwood. But in 1987, the Oregon Supreme Court forced the annexation of Rockwood into Gresham, against the sentiments of the people who lived in either place. So there sits Rockwood, excluded from Portland and never embraced by Gresham. A liminal place between two very distinct places.

You can find liminal places by going past the boundary of one place, but not yet arriving at another place.

The two cities of Portland and Gresham have deep animosity toward each other that goes all the way back to the founding of Oregon, so a shared vision of how to help Rockwood has never been in the cards. And to make matters worse, the school district line ran right through Rockwood east to west, and the city lines evenly bisected it north to south. Not one of the hospitals in the Portland metro area has Rockwood in its primary catchment area.

So nobody "owns" Rockwood. This liminal area does not exist on anyone's radar. Liminal spaces are rickety, spaces that are at risk of being subsumed by the larger, more powerful places adjacent to them. People who live in liminal spaces have a basic decision to make: On one hand, they could have the dominant adjacent community redefine them; on the other, they could rise to the challenge of defining themselves. Liminal spaces everywhere and liminal people in every culture are the engines of the new because they have to create—or die.

Since nobody in charge seemed to care much about Rockwood, I suspected that no one had bothered to describe it numerically. So I did it myself. Pulling the numbers from the US Census Bureau and other sites, I learned that life expectancy is a full ten years less in

Rockwood than in other parts of Portland. The reality is that life in Rockwood is alarmingly difficult. The homeless shelter that I used to be chairman of was not just full; it was turning away over 150 families every week. Each food distribution site had long lines, and there were homeless people in tents along the bike paths, outside the elementary-school fences, and below any building overhang that could shield them from the sleet. Violence, low educational attainment, obesity, low incomes, sex trafficking—all these are present in Rockwood. Numerically, Rockwood was the most distressed large community in the entire state of Oregon.

There's a reason I started with the numbers: Understanding place-based poverty begins with a statistical analysis. In just the past five years since I started my numerical examination of Rockwood, an amazing amount of place-based data has become publicly available. Place-based data has moved into "All I wanted was a drink of water and what I got was a firehose" territory as Big Data has finally achieved its promise of illuminating even the darkest corners of our cities. But when my quest began, these point-and-click resources weren't yet available. I had to mine the US Census Bureau data myself. But it was worth it, because the great benefit of census data is that it is so granular. Their data goes way beyond the county- or city-level data that you usually see in the media, or even the zip code data that I referred to before. Census Bureau data is available all the way down to the census tract level. A census tract has between 2,500 and 8,000 people or so living in it—about as granular as place-based data gets. Data at this level of detail brings neighborhoods into sharp relief. It's like moving from an old black-and-white TV to a 4K, ultra-high-definition screen. Details pop out that would have otherwise been fuzzy.

As an Oregon native, I knew my state well enough to know where to look for the poverty. Native American reservations were a good place to start. The vast rural areas were too, and perhaps a dying timber town or two. What I didn't anticipate was that Oregon's poorest community was right up the street from me. I knew that the Rockwood neighborhood was struggling because I was raised there. But Oregon's most needy?

It took me a while to understand why Rockwood's neediness was hidden to policymakers, the heads of the systems that serve it, and even the media. This racially and ethnically concentrated area of poverty is so geographically small that it shares a zip code with neighborhoods twice as rich. It's also nested in the city of Gresham, which was doing comparatively well. In Multnomah County, which is enjoying a historic boom, Rockwood didn't move the aggregate wealth needle.

The income disparities were stark. If the rich half of Multnomah County were a state, it would be the second richest state in America. And if the Rockwood half of Multnomah County were a state, it would be the second poorest state in America. Once I displayed this on the 4K data TV, I saw a community of forty thousand people who were the poorest, the most diverse, and the most violent in the state. People there had the lowest life expectancy (ten years shorter than people who lived just a few miles away), the worst health outcomes, and the lowest levels of educational attainment. Like the Pullman area of Chicago that I would visit later, Rockwood was at or below developing-world levels of human flourishing, and it was right in the middle of the wealthy and hot Portland market. Why was this okay with everyone? And how had I overlooked this? Surely everyone else knew—was I the only uninformed one?

I turned to the excellent materials in bookstores[1] to learn more. In most American cities, poverty has moved from the inner city to the suburbs. These neighborhoods form a ring around the core; they're frequently in collar counties or cities immediately outside the boundaries of a major city. Every American city has a Rockwood.

I learned later why this is, and at least in the case of Portland, the reason was shocking. But at this information-gathering phase, I was simply struggling with the realization that Rockwood even existed.

My struggle was more than an intellectual exercise. It was about Renaldo, the boy who knocked on my door on the day that local poverty wrecked my zen. As my information gathering continued, as I learned with increasing alarm about the toll of human sex trafficking in Rockwood, about the toehold that gangs from Los Angeles had in Rockwood, and about the developing-world-level of health outcomes, I got angry. Portlanders and their leaders were way more focused on the few homeless people on the street of the "good" part of town than they were on the tens of thousands of people nine miles away who were one missed paycheck from joining them. Portlanders pointed fingers at California or Texas for "busing homeless people into Oregon to take advantage of our liberal safety net," while the data proved that more than two-thirds of the state's homeless were homegrown, and that many of them came up from or passed through Rockwood.

Renaldo's story was not an isolated one. I had the data that proved that there were forty thousand Renaldos and no systemic plan to help them. As a Christian, I knew a moral imperative when I saw one, and this one was shaping up to be a big one.

I had to do *something*. I had crossed a line. I was not thinking at that point about forming a nonprofit or working on Rockwood full time. I was unemployed because the tech industry was in a downturn, but I was hoping to lead another company in the industry soon. But because of my efforts on behalf of nonprofits, I had easy access to the leaders in our area. *If I share with them about Renaldo, and income inequality, and the resulting desperate community*, I thought, *the leaders will thank me for my insights. And then I'll have fulfilled my responsibility.*

ARE YOU SEEING WHAT I'M SEEING?

The next week, I knocked on the office door of the quietest and most connected wealth manager in town. "Did you know that Oregon's poorest community is three miles from here, and no one is doing anything about it?"

Ed stared at me with his deadpan blue eyes and searched his mind's database. "That neighborhood needs serious work. You've got a lot of cleaning up to do before the land is able to be developed for nice apartments. You'd need to get those people out of there. Is that what you want to do?"

That was *not* what I wanted to do, I explained, because what he was talking about was intentional gentrification. The solution was not to get "those people" out. The lives that our neighbors were leading were full of pain in large part because the cost of renting an apartment was so high. When you are severely rent burdened, meaning that you are paying more than 50 percent of your income just to rent an apartment, then there is too little money left for food, clothing, education, insurance, a decent car, and other basic necessities. I wanted for someone to fix the problem, not simply to run the poor out of the community.

Next, I talked to the pastor of the largest church in town. He had only the vaguest notion of the folks in Rockwood. "I think some people who go to our church live there. I'd have to check the database. Why—do you want to start busing them here on Sundays or something?"

I explained that this was *not* what I wanted to do, because what he was talking about was forcing them into the regular church mold. I wanted instead for the church to do its thing in the neighborhood itself.

And I talked to the mayor of Gresham, who rarely set foot in Rockwood, even though it held 34 percent of his constituents. "The problem in Rockwood is that there is *too much* affordable housing," he said, "not too little. What we have done is concentrate poverty in a two-square-mile area. We need to get rid of the affordable housing and attract big businesses to the neighborhood. We need the tax revenue. Maybe you could bring in a Nike store or something." That, I explained, is *not* what I wanted to do, because it would be cruel. I wanted instead for the neighborhood to become vibrant and prosperous for the people who already lived there.

I kept looking for someone who would do something. But the banker wanted to extract wealth, the social service agency wanted to perpetuate dependency, and the hospital just wanted to get Rockwood people to stop clogging up their emergency rooms. There were more conversations, but they all started to sound the same. Surely Ed, the mayor, the pastor, and the others understood the problem, and yet they seemed to be blissfully and innocently unaware. Was there some mistake?

I was sitting on a precarious perch.

Or maybe there was a different problem. Maybe they were all so scared of Rockwood that they were paralyzed by fear. I recognized it in them because I knew something about that very feeling myself.

Ever since I earned my MBA from Northwestern University in 1994, I had driven hard in the telecommunication equipment industry. The press talked about how volatile Silicon Valley was in those days, but the software people had nothing on the telecom people. My industry was experiencing wild swings and wrenching change. In 2000 alone, *one million jobs* were wiped out when the bubble for telecom stocks burst. I thrived in this chaotic environment and became the CEO of a midsize manufacturing company by the time I was forty. It was true that I was a sought-after executive, but it was also true that I was sitting on a precarious perch. My whole career had been about driving out the uncertainty and gaining control of the messy ecosystem and the companies that it spawned.

The leading countries of the west, and especially America, have also been through a lot of chaos lately. Historians tell us that our current generation is facing more change than almost any other generation. We have more threats—both internal and external—to our way of life than I could catalog here. The US has assembled and repeatedly defended the largest empire that the world has ever known. But now we are beginning to dismantle our empire in order to share power with the rising global economy. US administrations will come and go, but the mega trend remains: The US is becoming relatively poorer, browner, and more culturally diverse. The tipping points are all around, and it feels to most white, middle- to upper-middle-class Americans that we have lost something that we will not regain. We seem to no longer be in control of the narrative, we no longer trust our map, and we do not know the way forward.

Many are hurt and confused by this. They really want to make America great again, and they think that it is possible. Others disagree and feel that America's map needs to be thrown away and a new identity pursued. All of us feel a powerful drive to gain (or regain) security. For America that means retaining control of the economic, political, and social systems that she runs on.

The Great Recession of 2008 dug deep into people, and its effects still linger today. Several of our friends lost their homes and their marriages. Nearly half of Americans, 40 percent, do not have even $400 that they could use in the event of an emergency. The assets that usually ensure retirement and stability are gone or severely limited. And whatever harm white people feel is felt twice as severely by African American people. Even people who did not understand subprime mortgages or the bank bailouts now understand that at the top of the system, mistakes are negotiable, while at the bottom of the system, mistakes are punitive. The government's response to the crisis has called into question the very idea that our economy works equitably for everyone. The response of larger businesses and higher-net-worth people has been to hoard cash and to hold onto assets that have appreciated in value rather than reinvest them. All across the vast landscape of America, people are at best, self-protective, and at worst, left without hope.

Paul Young is a best-selling author and a friend of more than fifteen years. One evening over chai tea, I told Paul that the people who were supposed to lead in Rockwood weren't leading. They were afraid that there was no solution to the area's deep problems and that things were only going to get worse. "How do we get through this?" I asked, frustrated and resigned.

Paul said, "Those who sit on a precarious perch rarely fly. They're fearful that the effort will cause the branch to break, so they freeze. *You're* frozen, Brad."

His answer irritated me. I wasn't frozen. I was in denial. People like me don't freeze. We don't experience the loss of identity or the loss of purpose. My people are American men—white, middle- to upper-middle-class, educated men—loaded with social capital, men who will bounce back. We have a world to run. We are Americans emboldened and empowered by Manifest Destiny, and we crush the dissenters and we defend the western canon of thought. The stability of the world depends on our currency, and our currency depends on trust, and our trust is built on conformity, and our conformity is built on force if needed. Don't tell us about identity and purpose. We invented identity and purpose.

But, still—Paul was right.

It was long past time for a beer with Ron Graves, my difficult friend. Ron is difficult because he always asks penetrating questions. Ron drives a truck for a manufacturer, paints abstracts, and still has the build of the rugby player he used to be. Now in his sixties, he's a cowboy poet whose soul feels like leather and coffee.

"Ronnie, the problem is that if I fall off my perch, I don't think that I'll ever climb back onto it again. I don't want to, because now

I don't think it's a perch worth having. So what am I supposed to do next?"

"I understand," he said. "It's looking more and more like the whole country is on a perch that's not worth having."

"But the thing is," I continued, "most of the folks who are doing well don't feel safe either. They're hoarding at levels that we've never seen in this country. They're stepping around homeless people and cutting funding for food for kids. Their retirement fund is all that they've got their eyes on, and too bad if their neighbor has a problem. You know that the rest of the world looks at us and thinks that we are brutal, don't you? Brutal, power-mad consumerists. The vastness of the gap between the rich and the poor is beyond understanding or fixing."

"So the disconnect has sunk in, has it?" he said. "Seems to me that the framework that served you pretty well for so long isn't working for you anymore. And you don't really want to put it right again. Can I ask you a question? What would happen if tomorrow you and I went down to Powell's?" Powell's is a famous bookstore in Portland that's a whole city block wide and five stories tall. I love to get lost in Powell's. "What if you loaded up all of your atlases and turned them in at the used book counter and came home with a journal?"

The road map doesn't describe where you are going.

"Wait…trade my atlas for a journ…oh, clever. Get rid of my road map and substitute blank pages. Draw my own maps. Chart my own course."

"Yeah. Your atlas stopped describing your journey a long time ago anyway. The map is not the territory."

"The map is not the territory? Then what is it?"

"It's an abstract. A map is an approximation of the territory. It tries to describe the territory, but it isn't the territory. When the territory changes, then the map has to be redrawn."

This struck a chord. The territory *was* changing, under my feet and under the feet of everyone else too. "Maybe it really is time to draw a new map."

"Just remember that a road map, no matter how accurate, doesn't describe where you are going. It can't. Where *you* are going, no one has ever gone before."

"So where *am* I going?"

Ron laughed. "I have no idea, brother. But I know something for sure. Paul and I are going there with you. You're not alone. There is hope. But that hope isn't found in making America great again. It's found in brokenness, silence, and reinvention."

> **Once our innocence is gone, each of us has no choice but to grapple with our newly revealed reality.**

Not long ago, I didn't know about the distressed community three miles up the road and the desperate families who lived there. I didn't know the history of racial discrimination, or crimes, or economic extraction that has plagued this area for over one hundred years. But I know it today, and I can't *not* know it anymore. That lack of knowledge was a form of innocence that I can't claim anymore. Thousands of people have come through Rockwood in these past seven years to hear me talk about my neighborhood, its assets, its needs, and its dreams. And when I give that talk, one of my objectives is to strip people of their naïve innocence. We may disagree on what to do, but we can still name reality together and agree on its contours. Once our innocence is gone, each of us has no choice but to grapple with our newly revealed reality.

THE BOX AND THE SOUP

A few weeks later, I shared all that I had learned with Kiesel. I told him that Rockwood was worse than anyone thought, and that none of our relief efforts were making things better. I told him that the leaders weren't leading because they were paralyzed by fear. I was starting to get angry. At who or at what, I wasn't sure.

"What you have encountered is the difference between the box and the soup," Kiesel said.

"The what and the what?"

"All of these people and organizations have a box. A church building, or City Hall, or a health clinic. In their view, people who want to be served need to come into that box. But out there, out in the neighborhood, is the soup. Tens of thousands of people who don't *want* to come into the box. Nobody knows who these people actually are. And the organizations who work in their boxes don't want to go out into the soup. Brad, who is in the soup in Rockwood right now?"

I could think of almost no one who was simply in the soup. The people who worked in the organizations—the teachers, pastors, government managers, and doctors—don't actually live in Rockwood. They live outside it and drive to their boxes—frequently an hour or more—to deliver services. Who were the leaders who were in the soup, knew the soup, and could engage with the soup? None of the leaders I knew did. But then again, neither did I. To my chagrin, I realized that in all of my research, I had not talked to anyone who actually *lived* in Rockwood.

"Sounds to me like you need to meet some real people," Kiesel said.

I nodded. "I'll do that. I mean, I'll at least explore. How deep could the rabbit hole get, anyway?

It didn't take long to learn that the rabbit hole got very, very deep.

CHAPTER TWO

Proximity

*M*y conversations with the mayor, the pastor, and the real estate developer had shown me that not everyone understood the problem the same way I did. More accurately, they understood the problem just fine but were frozen by the fear of falling off their perch. If I was going to really grasp what needed to be done, I would have to stop talking to the people fearfully defending their boxes. I needed to talk to soupy people.

I asked around, and a few names started to pop up. In every community, there are social entrepreneurs. In Rockwood, who were these entrepreneurs, and did they bring enough game to fix Rockwood's problems?

THE SOCIAL ENTREPRENEURS

Christine, an exuberant, feisty, six-foot-one, single African American woman who lived in a mobile home park right next to the train tracks, is one of our social entrepreneurs. My wife, Lynn, had met Christine at church and was inspired by what Christine was doing to help kids in her trailer park. The park has a large old farmhouse at its center that was available to the residents to use as they wished. Aware of the desperate need that the park's kids had for food and clothing, she had begun the year before accepting donations of clothes. Knowing that most of the kids in the run-down mobile homes were on their own all summer while their parents worked, she then started a day camp. She didn't charge any of the families that she served but instead asked them to volunteer their time in running her new charity operation.

I accompanied Lynn one day when she dropped off snacks for the day camp, and I was immensely impressed by what I saw: dozens of kids and a few parents interacting and having fun. Games, tutoring, health education. No governmental agency or church or school district or neighborhood association or nonprofit was involved. It was just Christine, receiving and giving with open hands. She was exhausted but happy.

How many other Christines were there in our neighborhood? As it turns out, there were lots. There was Dina, who opened a coffee shop in order to build community, and Mama Pat who lived across the street from the elementary school and took in kids who had no home to go to. Jennifer the Crusader, who wanted her neighbors to organize into We Are Rockwood (WAR—get it?). Maribel, who struggled to use the community-organizing skills she had learned in El Salvador to open a food co-op. Lina, who used an old school bus to distribute donated groceries. And Janet the Angry, who was always trying to get people to storm City Hall. These warriors didn't know each other, and each thought that she was the only one who was trying organically to meet the needs that she saw around her. Each of them appeared to be running successful interventions, because there were always tons of resources being donated to them, and lots of kids to give them to.

But as we got to know these heroes, we saw discouragement and even burnout. As gifted, tough, and resilient as they all were, they didn't have a leadership team, a nonprofit, or a financial base of support that could help them pay their bills. Those like Christine who were part of a local faith community were frequently misunderstood by their fellow parishioners and denied financial support. Eventually, I came to the reluctant conclusion that none of them stood any chance of scaling up their work sufficiently to change the equation for the neighborhood. As the years went by, one by one, these courageous women, feeling like failures, burned out and quit their passionate work.

But not all of Rockwood's social entrepreneurs were lone eagles. Perhaps teams would fare better. Lynn and I met up with Catherine and Cindy, middle-aged moms who lived in comfortable single-family houses that they owned in Rockwood. In other words, rare points of stability in an unstable place. But the apartments next to their cul-de-sac were going from bad to worse. No one had kept up with the landscaping, which had become a thicket of weeds and tall bushes that screened the activities inside. The parking lot had not been striped in years, so cars—whose they were no one seemed to know—were randomly parked, and some were broken down. There was litter everywhere, and the doors and railings were rusted. People came to one particular door all night long and stayed for only a few moments, a sure sign of drugs and perhaps sex trafficking.

"We tried talking to the police," Cindy said, "but they're already overwhelmed. Nothing was being done about this apartment, and Catherine and I couldn't do anything about it ourselves. So we did what our faith encourages us to do. We prayed. We walked every morning at 7:00 a.m. through the parking lot and prayed for the families inside the apartments."

"But you didn't know those families, did you?" I asked.

"No. I didn't know anyone who *did* know them. As we prayed our way across the parking lot, we would see them peek out their windows, then quickly shut the drapes if they caught our eye.

"After a few weeks, it occurred to us that we could also pick up garbage while we were prayer walking."

Over the next few years, I would hear over and over that people were doing the same thing: going on prayer walks with garbage bags in their hands. At first, it surprised me that people who didn't know each other were doing the same thing—praying and picking up garbage—but eventually I was hearing of it so often that it was no longer a surprise. A woman named Patti had been doing it on her own for thirty years.

"We got bolder and bolder," Catherine continued. "We would leave little notes on people's doors telling them that we were praying for them. We would also put little drops of oil on doorposts to invite protection."

"And did that work?"

"Yes. People began looking us in the eye and saying hi as they left for work. But then one day the manager came out, really pissed. He yelled, 'What are you stealing from my property?!' So I opened my bag and showed him that I was just picking up his own garbage. 'And you're pouring oil on the stairs so that people will slip and fall, and then I get sued. Get off my property!'

"We showed him that it was just a dot of oil," Cathy said, "and that it was up high—nowhere near the ground. Still, we honored his wishes and left. We were so discouraged. We were crushed, actually, that all of this effort had led to nothing."

So was that it? Just another story of neglect and discouragement? If people like Catherine and Cindy couldn't create neighborliness and personal interaction, then what hope was there for regular people?

"But that's not the end of the story," Cindy said. "About a week later, the manager mowed the yard. A crew removed the overgrown bushes, and the next month the parking lot was striped. Catherine and I doubted that he would get mad if we thanked him, so we walked over, breathed a prayer for courage, and knocked on his door."

"Did you hear a gun being cocked on the other side?"

"No! He was smiling when he opened the door. He told us that some of the residents had complained to him because he had run off those nice ladies. He told us that we were welcome back, as long as we didn't pour oil on the steps and make people fall. We agreed, and we resumed our prayer walks."

IT TAKES SOME BACKBONE

"I don't think that you or I could, or even should, be social entrepreneurs in the style of Christine, Catherine, and Cindy," I told Lynn. "They're wonderful. They are of their neighborhood. We aren't."

"True," Lynn said. "But could we *serve* them in some way? Such as by creating an umbrella organization, a collaborative or something, and make them part of something bigger. We could network them with other grassroots efforts for mutual support. We could aggregate their financial needs into one grant request. We wouldn't interfere in the relationships they have with their neighbors, but we could help them with resources and help manage their efforts for better results."

This new concept—seeing our work as an umbrella organization—became a major element to our strategy. I discovered that the terms used for organizations such as ours were ones like "backbone" or "hub." When backbones get big enough, they can become a region's anchor institution capable of quarterbacking the plays for the entire community.

But there was a problem. One does not just set up shop in a community and announce that one is providing leadership. One must be invited.

For the next three months, I did nothing but listen. I started with the pastors and school administrator that I knew and worked down long lists of referrals from them. By the time I was done nine weeks later, I had interviewed 116 soupy people. I learned what they thought of Rockwood, what their missions and visions were, how much money they had to work with, which groups and individuals they were trying to help, and what types of results they were achieving. I gauged whether they were receptive to a new hub organization. Later, I learned that there was a term for what I was doing: *asset mapping*. In the discipline of Asset Based Community Development, asset mapping is a key first step.

The assets that I discovered in Rockwood astonished me. We had more than ninety languages spoken at home in just a two-square-mile area. We were the youngest large community in Oregon, teeming with entrepreneurs and visionaries eager to get businesses started. And all of this was invisible to me and most community leaders because we were so disconnected.

It became clear to me halfway through the 116 conversations that if I was really going to understand Rockwood, I would have to be much closer to the people. You might think that people who live in the middle-class homes of America would understand the depths of poverty right in their communities, but they usually don't. I know that I didn't. Most of us learn about poverty in America through media: TV, movies, and even this book take the lived experiences of people who are affected by poverty and frame them for consumption by people who aren't. The message inevitably gets warped and abstracted. As a result, consumers who otherwise might be compassionate enough to want to do something about it feel sidelined. "I would like to get involved, but I don't know what to do" is the number-one comment I hear now when I speak to groups. "I don't know what to do" is the motto of the naïve innocent and the distant. People who are actually engaged in these neighborhoods, people in the soup, know exactly what to do.

What transforms "I don't know what to do" into meaningful engagement? In a word, proximity. Proximity recognizes that the yawning income disparity in the US is growing. Proximity understands that we do not understand. Proximity declares that it is no longer okay to let media mediate. Proximity means physically traveling to a low-income neighborhood and being physically involved. Proximity reduces my distance from the poor from miles to the width of a café table. And it means staying there for as long as it takes until I am more interested in the real you than I am in the idea of you.

> **Proximity means reducing my distance from the poor from miles to the width of a café table.**

When the distance is miles, we have the luxury of looking at our society through whatever lens we want and using whatever framework suits us, whether it is social or political or religious. But when we're close enough to look each other in the eye, we see each other for who we really are. We say, "Tell me your story." The framework becomes less relevant, and the reality of our shared experience comes alive.

When I finally saw my neighbors for who they really are, it hit me that who they really are is much more wonderful than I imagined.

For months I met my neighbors across café tables. I learned more and more about the bewildering array of support services for low-income families, but it didn't make much sense to me. I needed a framework on which to map these assets.

Dr. Peter Clark is one of the world's experts on poverty. He was a friend from our Wheaton College days, and he had gone on to a stellar career. I reached out to Peter, and although he was at his home in Madrid, Pete cleared time on his calendar. He listened to me struggle to make sense of Rockwood and then said, "Can I share with you the terms that we use? *Relief* describes those programs that spend aid dollars on specific felt and immediate needs. *Development* are those programs that spend on the bigger picture: the systems of health care, of government, of schools, of faith communities, of infrastructure and other categories that encourage people's abilities to naturally rise. *Relief* and *development* are two ends of a spectrum. There might be a stop in between called *betterment*, where we educate people on how to care for themselves."

"Peter, that's so basic but so helpful," I said. "If we only had the resources to focus on one of those, which is better? Development, right?"

"Well, they're all important. A cost/benefit analysis would tell you that the highest return interventions target specific things. Take public health. Malaria is a horrible, debilitating tropical disease that can be treated with pills. The World Health Organization knows the science, they know what does and doesn't work, and they've gone very deep with it. In globally certified factories, manufacturers produce the pills in huge volumes very cheaply. In something specific like this, these bigger organizations have the capacity to really produce results, and to do so at scale for pennies per intervention. Relief is all about alleviating specific unnecessary human suffering at scale—a million people at a time. In contrast, development is about promoting human flourishing more broadly."

"It sounds to me like most of what the organizations out here in Rockwood are doing is relief," I said. "Maybe some betterment too.

There must be eighty of them. It isn't as if they're asking for my help, because they aren't. Do you see any opportunity here for me, if I'm seeking to get involved?"

"I say go for the development end of the spectrum," he advised. "These 116 people you had conversations with are presumably delivering real results, but I think you could help them accelerate their impact. Let's keep in touch. You've got a steep learning curve in front of you."

I thought about that continuum between relief and development, with *relief* addressing immediate felt needs and *development* describing the systemic efforts needed to change the environment for families. And *betterment* describing someplace in the middle where people are growing their own capacity for improvement. I made that continuum the vertical axis on a chart, and for the horizontal axis, I created a continuum of relief or development efforts done *for* the poor, *for* our neighbors, *for* immigrants and refugees, versus those things done *with* low-income families, the immigrants, the refugees. I placed my 116 conversations on that grid. It was immediately clear that the vast majority of the efforts being made in Rockwood were basically *relief* efforts *for* the poor—efforts that showed up in the lower left-hand corner of my chart. *Development* efforts made *with* the families of Rockwood—those that showed up in the upper right-hand corner of my chart—were far fewer. The way that I could add value to the community, I concluded, was to drive resources from the lower left-hand corner to the upper right-hand corner. And that became and has remained our focus.

The chart I created looks complicated if you include all 116 efforts in Rockwood. But take out about one hundred of the programs, just for illustrative purposes, and the significance of the chart becomes much clearer:

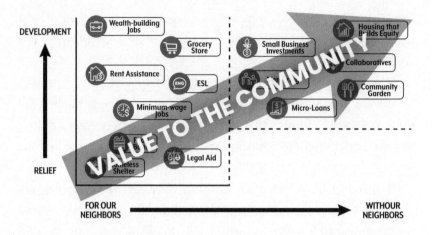

Did I feel angry that so much effort being expended in Rockwood, all of those programs showing up in the lower left of my chart, was failing to bring about lasting change? Sure. But I didn't feel any moral judgment against those organizations focused on that corner of the model. People who work exclusively in a relief world know that their intervention is needed. The third-grader needs his school backpack that is loaded with supplies because his parents will not be buying him one before school starts in September. But I was becoming more and more frustrated about why that same kid, in a year, as he enters fourth grade, will need another backpack full of supplies given to him. That child's situation did not improve during the year. Nor will it the year after. Or ever. That's one difference between relief and development.

I shared my findings with Kiesel. "So," I asked, "are these 116 organizations relevant to the needs of this disconnected, liminal community?"

"Well, sure. In their own way, most of them are doing their best with limited resources. The trouble I see is that the whole is not greater than the sum of its parts. It all feels disjointed and competitive. People in one organization don't know what other organizations are doing. Government is absent. People are pointing fingers. They're looking for help. And yes, that sounds like an opening for you. But you'll have to battle the existing community structure and its leaders if you're going to lead."

"What structure? What leaders? The county's coordinator for Rockwood said, 'Brad, everywhere I go, I am in a meeting full of coordinators. Where are the leaders?'"

Lynn was in the background during this conversation, cheering me on and expressing concern. She was just finishing her graduate Certificate in Public Health at Oregon Health Sciences University and was eager to start working in her field. She and I had always dreamed of working full time in relief and development when we got into our fifties, when our boys were out of the house, when I had achieved everything that I wanted to achieve. But now we were questioning that plan. If I didn't go back into tech, then should we start to work in Rockwood? If we did, how would we make a living? Would either or both of us actually find in Rockwood the significance and fulfillment we were looking for?

The prudent thing to do would be to set these questions aside and just go get a job. But in 2012, in the telecom equipment industry, there *were* no jobs. The equipment manufacturers I knew so well were shedding executives right and left. Some of the leaders of the companies on my list to call contacted me first and wondered if I had a safe port in the storm for *them*.

So there I was. I had driven tech as far as it could be driven and gained no more security or control than when I started as a young man. I was paralyzed. This was becoming a real crisis financially, and I needed to act. But as a seasoned entrepreneur, I also knew that I should have my financial backing in place before I kicked off the new initiative—especially a poverty initiative.

A few days before Christmas in 2012, I was telling Dr. Loren Sickles, my brother-in-law and an expert on community development, what

I was learning. Loren never offers an opinion unless I point-blank ask him for it—a trait I would like to see more of on social media. I was really troubled when Loren and I talked, because I was coming to the end of the evaluation process and was staring at the need to make a big decision. Would I start a new organization, or would I give up and move on?

"Well, everything you've told me sounds great," he said. "What's the problem?"

What's wrong, I told him, was that I was panicking. I had set a fund-raising goal of $30,000 by the end of the year, and I was at only $20,000 with no real prospects for a big gift to go over the target. We were broke, I told him, and starting a nonprofit without adequate backing was doomed to failure. Everything I had learned in business screamed that moving ahead, under the circumstances, was a bad idea.

"The rich and the powerful use 'compassion' as just one more tool to serve their political and financial ends," Loren said. "Your work comes from a different place: identification with the poor and the struggling. There will *always* be conflict at the heart of this work. Don't try to resolve the conflict. It is this very breach that authentic, vulnerable, and truthful community lives in."

I knew that Loren was right. Healing Rockwood would have to be done without adequate resources. The big systems were not likely to offer money for development work in Rockwood. Why? Because they live in a zero-sum world where if one group gets more grant dollars, then another organization gets fewer. I would have to bring *new* money, and unfortunately not much of it was lying around.

Loren changed the subject. "So if you don't have much money, what assets do you have?"

I rattled off the incredible assets I had uncovered in my research, some of which had little dollar value and some of which could be very valuable. I thought of the strength of the Slavic and Latino families and churches. I listed vast resources held by people and institutions immediately outside Rockwood that could be pointed inward. The infrastructure of the area—roads, mass transit, and so on—was excellent because of a recent investment in urban renewal. Lynn and I were assets.

"Good. Now what obstacles are there?" Loren asked.

"Where to begin? At the top of the list is that the dereliction of Rockwood suits the interests of the rich and powerful just fine. Just under that is a community that doesn't yet have the courage to rise out of its poverty of spirit. And to round out the list, Lynn and I are coming to this empty-handed neighborhood with empty hands of our own. We're terrified. We're ninety days behind on our mortgage. How can I commit to what will ultimately be a failed effort, followed by bankruptcy?"

What Loren said next floored me. "Brad, you can't *not* do this. Too many people are excited. Everyone I know is talking about what you are dreaming up. You have given people hope for the first time in decades."

You can't *not* do this. You have given people hope for the first time in decades.

If any of my other friends given to pep talks had said this, I might have shrugged it off. But Loren had never challenged me before, and he never has since. The call I felt toward serving in Rockwood came not just from Loren but from forces bigger than he or I. That was truly a turning point moment for me—then and there, I decided to say yes to that call, whether it meant demise or victory. And which of the two it would be, I had no idea. Lynn was not surprised. "I always knew that you would be driven to form the company and launch. I just wondered how long the skid marks had to be before you gave in. Just know this: I am completely, 100 percent with you."

Finally the grind was over, the decision made. I had found my own Calcutta. Neither the social entrepreneurs nor the system leaders were going to fix Rockwood. I had identified a gap that could be filled by a backbone organization. And I had decided to act. I filed the incorporation papers and wrote a business plan. We incorporated only ten weeks after I first thought of the Rockwood Community Development Corporation, and on Jan. 1, 2013, we began operations.

What happened next was explosive, challenging, wounding, and inspiring. The launch of the development corporation set the gears in motion not just for Lynn and me, but also for our beloved Rockwood. And the next eight years formed patterns that spelled out possibilities for liminal communities well beyond Rockwood's borders.

CHAPTER 3

Poverty, Inc.

*A*few weeks after agreeing with my brother-in-law that I *can't not*, I knocked again on the door of Ed, the real estate developer and wealth manager. I told him that Lynn and I had decided to start an organization that serves as a backbone to Rockwood's other aid organizations, and also develops housing there. "I need a ton of land and money," I said. Any idea where I can get it?"

Ed knew where all of the money in our county was hidden. "I know a guy who has some land that he could put into play. Do you have a business plan I can show him?"

I did, indeed. After talking to 116 people and learning that few resources in Rockwood went toward what we called *development* in the previous chapter, I was ready to describe reality. My plan laid out the vision, the mission, and the tagline of the new effort. Through all of the ups and downs of the next years, those concepts haven't changed and still serve as my guide star. Here's what I came up with:

Tagline: Working together to make a place where everyone can learn, earn, and belong.

Vision Statement: We dream of communities:

- with rising levels of prosperity;
- where employment and decent housing are accessible by all;
- where health outcomes are excellent;
- where vibrant community life emerges from diversity; and
- where all show compassion to those in need.

Specifically, our **mission** entails:

- Expanding the supply of decent housing;
- Supporting economic development;
- Increasing access to health care and encouraging healthy behavior;
- Creating and sustaining public-private partnerships;
- Aligning the strategies and resources of the educational, faith-based, governmental, capital, social service, business, and health care sectors.

Writing the business plan made me put down on paper some terms that we all know but rarely need to use with precision.

Community is just a geographically bounded set of relationships. Knowing your boundaries means that you are not in a vacuum. You are in a context. You know that your neighbors' lives are lived in relationship to a specific place that has housing, offices, markets, roads, parks, neighboring communities, transit, and clinics. You also know the cultural environment like families, equity, clans, jobs, schools, churches, agencies, clubs, the presence or lack of digital access, diversity, in and out migration, history, justice, government, and the degree to which the neighborhood is relevant to the larger community that it sits adjacent to.

Poverty is the result of broken relationships between individuals and their context. We humans are products of our environment and of our perceptions of relative well-being. That contributes significantly to our overall sense of flourishing. As individuals in the community restore right relationships, they eventually reduce poverty or other unnecessary forms of suffering.

My plan put *place* at the center of the strategy. And every group, individual, program, or policy that impacted that place was therefore a part of the plan. I created the organization with an Oregon-wide charter and invented the legal name Community Development Corporation of Oregon. Its initial focus was a two-square-mile area, so our street name (a "doing business as" or dba) was the Rockwood CDC. My thought was that if we were ever to work in another town, say Bend, we would call that work the Bend CDC. This would allow us to feel local where it mattered, but also to have the heft of a large organization where it mattered.

WHAT IS A "HOLISTIC" APPROACH?

My plan also put a *holistic approach* at the center of the strategy. By that I meant I was developing a geographically bound set of relationships. More plainly, in trying to fix things, I was concentrating on one zip code—Rockwood's.

Holistic means trying to put all aspects of society to work on the common goal—the businesses, the government, the health systems, the schools, the faith centers, the media, and our neighbors. The results are holistic too: better health, higher income, less violence, greater educational attainment, healthier families, and so on. Holistic thinking means that each of these elements can no longer be understood as standing alone. Each must be understood in its relation to the whole.

What are the holistic issues facing Rockwood? And what capacities within the community can I build on in addressing those issues? To answer that question, I thought it was time to check in again with Dr. Peter Clark, who had helped me understand the world of relief and development.

When I told Peter what I wanted to do, he lit up. "Brad, you need to do holistic—no question. In nonprofit work, holistic isn't normal, and that's why you'll really have an impact. Assessing community flourishing in a comprehensive way is complex. Most people working in this field don't even try. Remember the old saying, 'If all you have is a hammer, then every problem looks like a nail'? Well, the work done in most organizations is closely related to the technical skills the organization has. For example, I regularly consult with a huge organization that does microloans to small businesses. The leaders of the organization are all bankers. They see everything the organization does as *financial inclusion*, the banking term for *getting more clients*.

Holistic puts all aspects of society to work on the common goal.

Bankers are hardwired to see their business, and their clients, in that way. But if a banker were to say, 'Oh—it's not just the loan that will get people out of poverty, it's the social capital created by having people meet together, or it's the bad habits you prevent people from having, or its actually conversion, through which their souls are healed,' then the design of that organization's microloan program would change greatly."

"Peter, I can understand how holistic thinking would be effective and easily apply to a Filipino fishing village of four hundred people, because the limited geographical area would let you measure and understand each element of the built environment and the culture. You can impact the community with pinpoint accuracy. Your change model can be refined using statistical means. But how does that same approach work in the US? It seems crazy when you're talking about forty thousand people in the middle of Portland who come from all over the world."

"How many languages are spoken at home in Rockwood?"

"The school districts have counted over ninety, making it one of the most diverse areas in the United States. Each of the cultures reflected by those ninety languages will have a different concept of what human flourishing looks like."

"Wow," Peter said. "Working holistically in that context will be difficult. And there aren't a lot of examples to guide you, because there isn't a lot of thinking about this going on out there. But you'll find the task less difficult if, from the beginning, you frame your task holistically."

"So how do I define holistic human flourishing?"

"Let's start with a definition. Flourishing means health, prosperity, peace, safety, justice, and other elements. This is not a new idea. Thousands of years ago, Jewish writers coined the word *shalom*, which we usually just translate as "peace." But the word *shalom* is much more than that. It is about wholeness, completeness, and restoration of justice. I think of flourishing, or shalom, in terms of five areas: peace with self (which includes self-esteem, hope, attitudinal predisposition, overcoming addiction, overcoming bad habits, and mental health), peace with family, peace with community, peace with the natural environment, and peace with God."

"Wait a minute. We're not creating a religious organization here."

"No, and you shouldn't. Yet all of the research shows that we are hardwired in such a way that spiritual values need to be addressed. To rise out of poverty, people have to have hope in the future."

The more I talked to Peter, the more convinced I was that a holistic organization was what I needed to create. I realized that when it came to wholeness—to shalom, as he called it—if I was not doing it *all*, then I wasn't doing it *at* all. It dawned on me that

Peter was using the term *holistic* in the same way we used the term *ecosystem* back in my technology days.

Holistic or *ecosystem* thinking isn't very common in relief work. But I'd seen it used to great effect once—during the year that I ran a big nonprofit in the Philippines. This mega organization that worked with a hundred thousand ultra-poor Filipinos every year could, in fact, "do it all" on a small scale as well—say, for a village of four hundred people. As a US executive used to leading a company with a singular focus and careful elimination of extraneous parts, this sprawling organization felt alien but exhilarating. I learned later that there's a term for this approach: *wraparound*, meaning that my organization was pretty much providing everything a poor family would need in order to move forward.

> **Look at flourishing, or shalom, in terms of five areas: peace with self, peace with family, peace with community, peace with the natural environment, and peace with God.**

In the US, a single organization trying to provide wraparound services would have to be too massive and multidisciplined to be practical. But if a *network* of smaller, more specialized organizations could together do everything that families need, then we might be able to achieve the same results.

In Rockwood, the answer would be in partnering, in collaboration, and in bridge building. If I were to lead that effort, I couldn't be identified with any one ideology or outcome or change model, any more than the commissioner of the NFL could show favoritism to any one team. I would have to be neutral, perhaps even bland, if I were to be accepted by each of the specific organizations as noncompetitive. I also knew that I could not simply identify myself as the backbone service organization for Rockwood. That identity would have to be bestowed upon me by the community. And that wouldn't happen unless they realized deep down that they had more to gain than lose by working collaboratively.

So there it was. The business plan I'd written held all of our core concepts, and people with resources wanted to see it. I had no idea until I released it to curious people that they would receive me as a conquering hero.

START YOUR ENGINES

Just two weeks after I'd released the business plan, one of the local mega churches invited me to speak briefly from stage about my plans. This church would occasionally allow what amounts to an extended announcement about some new service opportunity, followed by an invitation for people to sign up at a table in the foyer after the service. I was excited about this, because if the CDC were to actually work, we would need a lot of money and a lot of people. At this point, we had neither, and it was much easier to imagine that everyone would continue to not give a rip about poverty than it was to imagine that they would.

As Lynn and I headed out the door that Sunday morning to make my announcement, I suddenly felt that I should grab a yellow legal pad so that anyone interested in helping could give me their contact information. I called my friend Travis and asked if he would be at that service. "I might need you to help out," I told him.

I made my three-minute announcement, then went to the foyer to wait for the service to let out. An hour later, the double doors opened and people streamed out as usual. But what was *not* usual was that they were heading for me! As in a wish-ful-fillment movie, they crammed around the table wanting to sign up. They were crowded two deep, then three, then four. So many wanted to tell me or Lynn or Travis their heartfelt story of suffering in Rockwood. *What can we do?* they wanted to know. The trouble was, we had no idea ourselves what any of us should do. We didn't have a program. Or an office. Or a website, or even a phone number. We were just us.

But after this same mob scene happened in three services at that church, all on that same weekend, we had about two hundred volunteers and donors signed up!

Later that Sunday, I sat down and looked through the pages of contacts and notes. I was thrilled, of course, but—what was I supposed to do with all of these people? I was also, frankly, pretty pissed off that this level of pent-up demand to do something had existed for so long. Was this why the summons I felt on my life to do something was so strong?

In subsequent weeks, this mob scene was repeated over and over. If I was to build the CDC as the fabled villagers in the folk-tale about stone soup concocted their pot of soup, then I needed to engage with these villagers who all wanted to add their little bit to the pot. It was exciting and gratifying for sure. But without a system—a system that I believed I could provide—all that would ultimately occur was a failure.

I hate to admit it, but I soon stopped accepting speaking invitations because I would walk away with so many "you ought to call this person" and "have you applied to this foundation" that I couldn't possibly follow up on more than a small fraction of the leads. And what started eight years ago has not let up to this day. I and the rest of the CDC team receive many leads, inquiries, offers, and connections every day. Every day. These "bottoms up" assets are not just powerful, they are essential to an asset-based approach to community development.

Ed passed along my business plan to this old friend. The friend owned five acres in the heart of Rockwood that had gone derelict. That acreage was not just emblematic of the decay of Rockwood. It *was* the decay of Rockwood. This Disneyland of human deprivation had a strip club, a check-cashing store, an hourly motel, and a couple of run-down businesses with leaking roofs. It was trash-strewn and dangerous. It wasn't that Ed's friend was a bad person; he wasn't. But he had let decades of neglect turn his once-thriving land into a nightmare. It wasn't that he wanted a strip club. It's that the club used to be a pretty good Mexican restaurant, but when times got hard in 2008, the restaurant brought in girls to attract customers. In Oregon, stripping is a protected free-speech right, and there's no way to shut it down. In fact, for the owner of the restaurant to turn it into a strip club, she didn't even have to get a permit just as long as she was still selling food. When stripping didn't pay the bills, she brought in video poker. And when that didn't bring in enough money, she sent the girls out onto the busy sidewalk wearing tiny clothes and big signs to advertise lap dances.

The same afternoon I got word from Ed about his friend's property, I hopped into the car and drove over to check it out. The drive there looked more familiar the closer I got, and eventually I realized to my astonishment that it was right across the street from Renaldo's house. The very place that connected Renaldo to the drug trade that had abused him was the strip club. I met with the owner and learned that the land was worth $2.5 million, and that he was interested in donating it! I mean, all nonprofits start with a $2.5 million donation and hundreds of volunteers, right? As the weeks went on, however, it became clear that this friend did not actually have a charitable motivation and in fact still needed income from the property. Although I believe we could have met his needs and wants even within a nonprofit context, I tore up the letter of intent and instead created a for-profit business that could accomplish the dual tasks of giving him and his descendants income and also redeveloping the neighborhood.

Offers big and small began coming in faster than we could respond to them. Rev. Jason Albelo, who knew that despite the growing excitement about something meaningful happening in Rockwood, Lynn and I still had very real financial needs, said, "Brad, my church will step up with $3,000 a month for three months. Is that enough to keep you and Lynn in the game? Don't pull the plug just because the people with resources are slow to give. Let them rise. Then the neighborhood will rise. And so will you and Lynn."

What a word at just the right moment. Three thousand dollars per month for three months would indeed give us three months of runway to get our little plane off the ground. What would happen on day ninety-one was anyone's guess, but the gift was real (and much appreciated) nonetheless. If I was going to impact the community, then I would have to believe that I had all the capabilities and resources that I needed for the next step. No more than the next step, but also—no *less* than the next step.

Things were moving fast. From the day I was told that I *can't not* do this until the day I had a $2.5 million development project, a business plan, two corporations, media attention, $12,000 in cash donations, and hundreds of volunteers was thirty-two days. It was exhilarating to be in demand, but it was an awful lot for someone as flimsy and imperfect as me to take. The truth was, I didn't *want* to move this fast. I was very familiar with the normal thinking in the tech world that you want to get to large scale and fast growth. But community development is different. Efficient, high-scale growth too soon is probably a bad thing. It means, inherently, that the existing systems (which have already failed the community) are being reinforced, because scale, speed, and practicality are about keeping those systems in place. Instead, I wanted to start with small scale and slow growth as I brought everyone down the path together. Growth could become big and fast later, perhaps once the systems had been challenged by new ones.

The motto I was trying to follow was an old familiar one: *If you want to go fast, go alone. If you want to go far, go together.* This focus on collaboration is summed up in one of our four core values: *Build bridges, not armies.* This is the ethic of inclusion, making sure that we are connecting the disconnected and not taking sides. We are not using our resources to reinforce bad systems. This core value calls for a different kind of leadership than I was used to. Bridge Builders show neutrality, relatability, and vulnerability. They receive with open hands, and they give with open hands. Army Builders come into a community to accomplish a specific, usually numeric goal. Whether it is souls won or votes cast or members signed up, Army Builders view other organizations as a means to an end. Only Bridge Builders view other organizations as partners and collaborators.

Our Four Core Values	
It's Personal	Everyone who works with us and for us is personally involved in the lives of our community. This keeps us relationally connected to our neighbors and community. We intentionally invest in relationships as we invest in other aspects of community development.
Build Bridges, Not Armies	Everything we do is built on an ethic of inclusion, diversity, and justice. Reconciliation is hard work, and we are committed to building diverse relational bridges that lead to true justice.
Reconciliation	We pursue the disconnected and bring them into relationship through what is often hard relational work rooted in listening, humility, and learning.
Never Leave the Table	We are here for the long term, even when things get hard. We do not launch programs and then leave. Rather, we are here till our vision has been accomplished.

STORM CLOUDS APPROACH

This was when the first signs of resistance to our plans showed up. We couldn't know at the time that what we first thought were little annoyances would turn into an all-out war.

One of the warning signs was the presence of gatekeepers. These organizations and people were protecting the status quo from challengers like me. Four large community development corporations had been established in Portland for decades, and they had formed a tight and stable little ecosystem where everyone knew how big the pie was and who got the biggest piece. The affordable housing industry enjoys huge profit margins and virtually no risk. I naively thought that I would be welcomed into the club as one more person with good intentions, but instead I discovered that I was considered a threat to their stasis just for walking into the room. People in those development corporations assumed incorrectly that some federal, state, or local agency had asked me to launch our CDC. "If the city thought they needed another CDC," one leader sniffed, "they should have asked me first." The club was so good at keeping me out that it took seven years before we began winning federal funds for building housing.

The housing club wasn't the only group that resisted my efforts to launch a holistic nonprofit. Some politicians, social service agency heads, and landowners weren't going to easily give up the hold they had on their corner of the landscape. Clearly, for many people who felt some personal investment in the status of the community, the decline of the old and the beginning of the new in a liminal space feels like risk of loss more than it feels like life.

And some regular residents were against us too. Shortly after we set up a phone number, I received a voicemail from an anonymous caller:

> I am calling about the Rockwood whatever-you-call-it. I am really resentful that this is a discriminatory program that

is just for immigrants. If this was a white thing, it wouldn't be allowed by law. I am sick and tired of people, kids, children born in this community getting less benefits than those who come here by choice, and I just think that this is really wrong. You're just concentrating immigrants in one part of town, and Gresham is sick of it. We've got more than our share of it, and with it comes people who do not respect the law and all of that ... Our property values are going downhill, and this is wrong. So wrong.

Lynn, too, was out there talking to leaders and exploring how we would launch. One night she said, "So many of the elders who are supposed to be running the systems and the businesses that benefit our neighbors seem unhappy that we are setting up our practice."

"I know!" I said. "All we're doing is talking about the current, observable reality in Rockwood. We're not making anything up. We're discovering the heart of this community, and that **Hope is an indictment of cynicism.** is churning up *fear* in those who've borne some responsibility for responding to needs here."

"These people are blind to how much their actions on behalf of Rockwood are actually motivated by self-interest, self-preservation, and self-dealing, and it's been going on for a long time. There's much going on here that I don't understand, but I can see that they feel I'm challenging their dominance just by asking questions. My presence alone is the challenge."

"Well, we are focusing on possibilities, right?" I said. "On gifts and on generosity? Hope itself is an indictment of cynicism. Our hands are open to freely receive and freely give. These other groups have closed hands. They've kept a lot of others out too."

"Right," Lynn said. "It's a little bit wild. *So many* organizations, and entrepreneurs, and faith communities, and county and state agencies are just looking for a home. They wonder why they are kept out of Oregon's poorest community. They all want to know what our change model is."

"So what do you tell them?" I was genuinely curious, because I wasn't completely sure what our change model was myself.

"I make it fuzzy on purpose," she said. "It's more important that we all find a place to belong than it is that we all work in lock step. Is it fair to call it a change model when all we're doing is opening up the windows and letting fresh air in? Letting the community itself define the outcomes? I don't think that organizations whose bottom-line interest is self-preservation know how much pent-up demand there is to *do something* in Rockwood."

Given the explosive first thirty-two days of our existence, even these whiffs of resistance were enough for me to consider quitting. It's not that the bad guys were formidable. It's just that I was so weak. And frankly, I was confused by my own dramatic journey and unsure sometimes why I was choosing to be accountable to my community at all. Why would I carve out space for new life and defend it against brutal attack when necessary? Why would I work so hard to bring marginalized people into the center? I know the answer, and I know how to state it clearly, but the answer is tough for many people to hear because it's so countercultural. People in American culture thirst for heroes, and we deeply believe that when our need is great, a man on a white horse will ride in to save us. Our love for heroic leaders creates a hierarchical agenda that we benefit from and drowns out our ability as a group to imagine and create a new future.

Over the years, the media has often wanted to write in their stories that I am that man on the horse. I wouldn't go along with it. On one occasion, I told them, "If you're interested in our English language school, then I would be glad to introduce you to a Pakistani mom with a fascinating backstory, and she can tell you about her journey to acquire English. That, and not me or my team, is the story." I knew that, sadly, the journalist wouldn't be interested, and that the mom's story would never be told. If you've ever tried to get the media to reframe a story once they've decided on their slant, you understand the problem. In this case, they treated the school and its founder like the news and the Pakistani mom like a human-interest story. In reality, it's the reverse. The Pakistani mom is the news, and I might be (at best) a human-interest story. The good and real news is that she is envisioning a future for her children centered on their flourishing, and that she is doing it right here in this liminal place. She is part of a group of students crafting a new future that—who knows?—could eventually impact our whole nation. What counts is that once she masters the nuanced difference between the English words *resident* and *citizen*, she could shift our world on its axis.

> **No one is coming to save our country's liminal neighborhoods.**

No one is coming to save our country's liminal neighborhoods. They never have, they never will, and that is not what I did. At best, I brought compassion and a sense of justice—perhaps good business skills—but a lot of people have those qualities. I really don't think that the explanation for my deep commitment to Rockwood and its people lies in my positive attributes. Instead, I think that it lies in the absence of negative ones. By that I mean that my consumerism was sheared out of me when my company collapsed and I was financially wiped out. My isolation was stripped away when I had to rely on friends to carry us along. My need for retribution against adversaries vanished when I saw how big the possibilities were for human flourishing. I was no longer enamored with top-down, numbers-based leadership because I saw how it snuffs out culturally authentic leadership. So if you take a functional adult and subtract the Americanisms, what do you get? A neighbor.

Three years after Lynn and I formed the Rockwood CDC, I was sitting in a large conference room with thirty representatives of organizations in the social services sector. I was part of a collaborative that was trying to redesign how social services were delivered in Rockwood. The work was daunting, and this particular meeting had stalled. The gifted facilitator stopped and posed an energy-giving challenge. "Let's go around the room, and I would like each of us to use just four words to describe why we are committed to this collaborative." As we did, each would say good things like "excellence in addiction recovery" or "making the system efficient" or some other worthy value. When my turn came, I realized that I was the only one in the room who could truthfully utter the most powerful answer: "They are my neighbors."

My "why" contained no expectation of return. I was not bartering with anyone. My commitment was not conditional upon results. I was not dependent on a small group of wealthy and powerful people to redirect their resources to me. I was simply attentive to and responsive to the voice of my community. I became a neighbor.

What happened next set the stage for booming growth and triggered a showdown of systems in the governor's mansion.

CHAPTER 4

Things Get Real

*T*here was one more knock at the door. A couple apologized for being late and ducked in out of the rain. "Is this where the staff meeting is for the … uh, corporation thing?"

I stared at them blankly. I didn't recognize them. They were welcome to find a seat in our living room, of course, but there was a problem. There were already eighteen people there, and now with them, twenty. Twenty people at our first "staff" meeting! We had met so many people in the first thirty-two days and had invited them all to "join staff."

We went around the room and introduced ourselves. There were people there from so many different stages of life: young couples exploring non-corporate careers, students pursuing advanced degrees in development, retirees yearning to fill their time meaningfully, and even mid-career people cut adrift by the Great Recession. It was a roomful of white, middle-class or upper-middle-class, educated adults in transition in their lives—up, down, or out an exit.

We had no money to pay staff, of course, but then none of the people now crowding our living room needed money as urgently as Lynn and I personally did. Instead, these people needed something far rarer: purpose. And we had that in abundance. Years later, as I coached other young community development startups, I would see that this experience is part of the pattern. Distressed communities everywhere have a pent-up demand for someone to *do something*. When a new leader simply opens a door for volunteering or donating, the response is tremendous.

An all-volunteer organization has strengths and it has weaknesses. One weakness is that the only people volunteering initially were from my own culture. Also, it's trickier to manage people when they're not working for a paycheck. But what I would lose in internal control was more than made up for by the passion that each volunteer brought. A great volunteer culture can accomplish more than a paid one. Creating and maintaining this culture would eventually be one of the strongest skills we would develop.

After the lengthy introductions, I said, "I got this call from someone at the county who had an idea for us." One of the retirees shifted uncomfortably in her seat. I knew that even mentioning our liberal county to this conservative retired schoolteacher would raise some resistance. "Oregon's first lady is concerned about poverty," I continued. "The governor's office has tasked the county with launching an anti-poverty program, and they're looking for a neighborhood to launch it in. Since we are the poorest community in Oregon, they would like to do it here. And they want to partner with us to do it."

"Wait," a recently laid-off software programmer said. "The governor wants *us* to do a major program? There's no way. We don't have the capacity to do anything. This is our first team meeting. We barely even *exist*! What are they thinking?"

I knew that he was right. We had no systems, no policies, and no bank account. The board was Lynn, one friend, and me. Our 501(c)(3) application hadn't even been approved yet.

"Why isn't the governor using the existing anti-poverty groups?" he asked.

"Because they don't trust them," I said. "This new program is all about building the social capital of our neighbors—exactly what we want to do. The existing programs are all about relief. Those agencies are nasty to and about each other, especially in what they say to the governor's office. Something high profile like this is a prize that most of them would shiv their grandmothers for. I think it's coming to us because we are the first people to open the window and let fresh air into this stuck community."

The program the governor's office wanted us to run was based on the concept of social capital. *Capital* is another word for *asset*— something that has value that can be spent. "Social capital" is a measure of how much capacity a person has to function well in, and benefit from, society. More tangibly, it's knowing who can help you, who you belong with, and who you can help. It's having a model for your kids to follow that gives them the opportunity to be better off than you. It is being interdependent; it is belonging somewhere. It is being at peace with your community. People low in social capital are isolated, afraid of their violent community. "For two years," a mom who lived in a low-income apartment told me, "I would not let my kids go out and play. There was nothing but scary people out there." That is the voice of low social capital.

Social capital is an imprecisely defined term in the field of development because there are at least two slightly different ways in which it is used. One refers to building up the internal bonds in a community, and the other emphasizes the bridging bonds that link the community to larger communities. In future years we would launch the nationally recognized Rockwood Speaks! program that creates bonding social capital. But this program sought to build bridging social capital. This meant recruiting and organizing three different types of people: first, our low-income neighbors who lack the social assets that they need to flourish. Second, our high-income neighbors and our systems leaders who possess these social and financial assets. And third, volunteers who are doing okay in their lives who will serve as trained navigators to connect the neighbor to the asset. The theory and the program design were academically sound, and we were excited about taking the lead on its rollout. If it went well in Rockwood, then the governor's office would roll it out statewide.

"So what do we do?" asked the practical and administrative-minded, young stay-at-home mom sitting on the floor of our living room.

I explained that we were to create this network and launch it in a one-day event. It already had a name, courtesy of the governor's office: the Opportunity Community. The state's commitment to its funding partners was to launch the program about six weeks from the day of our first staff meeting. They were offering us $15,000 to coordinate this, a gold mine for me. My new team jumped at it. But while they thought that it was possible that we could pull it off, they also thought it was unlikely. Someone knew about a gym we could use for the launch event. Someone else set up a spreadsheet and entered the names of the hundreds of volunteers and recruit navigators. Others knew where we could get food, graphic artists, and free printing. It looked as if we could indeed pull it off, so I called my contact in the county office and committed my new team.

Six weeks later, we held our first conference. Over 150 people attended, including the governor and his partner. We had identified and trained fifty navigators already, as well as one hundred neighbors who needed navigation and connection to asset-rich people from outside the neighborhood.

At the center of this structure sits the navigator, the one with the skills and knowledge to navigate the systems but who is not a case manager. Case managers make existing systems more effective; their function is making sure that the people who enroll in a given intervention, support, or treatment program use it effectively. Navigators are in the soup, finding the disconnected, and connecting them to a given intervention, support, or treatment program. They form relationships with their struggling neighbors and help them take the next step—as the neighbor defines it—toward wholeness. Many navigators don't know that they are navigators, because this is just how they live their lives. They are natural networkers. They might be a little nosy, but that comes from a heart of love, not judgment. When their neighbors encounter a barrier, the natural navigator just knows how to overcome it. Navigators are an indispensable component of functioning communities. I don't know what percentage of a given population are natural networkers, but I do know from the Opportunity Community event that I had no trouble finding fifty of them.

Some systems are waking up to the powerful role that navigators play in holistic community transformation. In medical systems, community health workers are hired and trained to pay attention to the built environment and to work with the neighbors who are hurt by it to change it. Many faith communities have chaplains charged with spending their time not in the church building but in homes, businesses, and the street meeting people where they are and directing them to spiritual resources.

Debi was scared. When she trained to be a navigator, she felt that she didn't have much to offer. *Everyone is talking about how they can connect neighbors to jobs and to schools, and I do nothing like that*, she thought as she took her seat at the table. *I'm just a grandma who works at the Sheraton and has lived in the neighbor-hood for twenty-five years.*

Soon Debi met up with a young couple who had recently emigrated from the tiny Pacific island of Chuuk. (The populations of Chuuk and Rockwood are about the same.) This couple was having a hard time navigating their new world. Debi discovered that there were other Chuuk emigrants working as housekeepers at the Sheraton where she worked. Yesterday, the young emigrant wife applied for her first job at that hotel. Debi also knew that the school in her neighborhood that taught skills to construction workers would accept the young man. "Just like that, I was helping this couple," Debi said, amazed. "Although I wouldn't have thought it, I ended up being the perfect person to help them achieve their goals. I couldn't be more thrilled!"

> **The poor are not the beneficiaries of Poverty, Inc. They are the raw materials. The beneficiaries are the people who run Poverty, Inc.**

We created about forty similar capital-building relationships among people.

As thrilling as this was, problems soon arose that surprised me. In subsequent years, we would see these problems arise again and again. But that first time, we were puzzled and alarmed. One of the challenges was that there was a huge mismatch between white upper-middle-class expectations and reality. I tallied a cost of $50,000 in cash and gift-in-kind to put on this one-day conference, which is wildly out of line with the resources of Oregon's poorest community. Another was that, somehow, the $15,000 that had been promised never materialized. That's because at each step along the way, from the funding source to the state to the county to the training organization, and then to me, a percentage was deducted for processing. Although no one took a very big bite, by the time it got to us, there was nothing left. Here we were, the start-up community-based organization with nothing and no budget, watching all of the well-funded groups siphon the funds. Another challenge was that the training organization was disorganized and ill-prepared for helping us actually run a network in the real world. But the biggest concern was that, although the training worked well for intergenerationally poor whites, it was less effective for people of color. One Latino woman summed it up well for me: "That white lady teacher sure knows a lot about white poverty. But I'm not so sure that she knows about me."

As a result of these challenges, I told the governor, the county, the training organization, and all of our partners that we would continue to support the Opportunity Community if someone financially supported the work and if we fixed the training with culturally relevant material. If those conditions weren't met, we would pull out for now. I learned in later years that few organizations in this line of work lay down ultimatums like this, because they themselves are operating from a poverty mindset that says that they should play the game. But from the beginning, we were more likely to confront the systems because we saw that the poor were really not the beneficiaries of those systems. Rather, they were the raw materials. And this time, I was too.

This idea that poverty-fighting is a system of its own is an important one. Poverty alleviation and relief efforts are so large that they actually form an industry. Isn't that something? I did not realize that the tens of billions of dollars that flow every year have produced millions of nonprofits, philanthropies, consultants, educational institutions, buildings, information systems, websites, and career tracks. Together, they form such a giant machine that people have started calling it "Poverty, Inc." There was a documentary released in 2014 that showed this industry in great detail, and that shocked many who understood it for the first time. When an organization focuses more on maintaining their business than on eliminating suffering, they are a part of Poverty, Inc. I was very concerned that a program like the one that we had launched was dancing very close to the line. I was alarmed enough to pull out.

Pulling out was not what Oregon's first lady had in mind. The Opportunity Community model was flawed, perhaps to the point that it could not be saved. I had dropped it pending our three conditions being satisfactorily met, and no other groups in Oregon were willing to put up with the mess our group had put up with that first time. The training organization was livid because years of lobbying had ended in embarrassment, and they would not take no for an answer. So the first lady called a summit meeting to hash things out. I had never been to a summit meeting, and I didn't know what there was to hash out. All that this massive effort had accomplished was draining my small reserves. Because I had entered into this work with open hands and an empty wallet, I had nothing to defend, no outcomes to chase, and no one to answer to.

> **Poveteers make a living off of the deficiencies in a community.**

Mahonia Hall is the beautiful 1924 Tudor Revival mansion that all of Oregon's governors live in while in office. The living room is stately but not too formal and has a baby grand piano that I was able to play before anyone else arrived. The room has one stained glass window in the shape of Oregon and another whose design is the state's seal. The First Lady, the training organization, a major social services agency, Multnomah County officials, and Lynn and I gathered for what was supposed to be a friendly chat. For the next hour I heard frustration and anger from the training organization because I had wrecked their careful rollout plan. I heard admiration from the county for how I was being evidence-based in assessing the success of the launch. I heard sniping from the social service agencies who had resources but would not use them unless they were later reimbursed. And Lynn and I expressed anger because we knew that if our nonprofit were to last and have impact, then we would have to keep digging deeper than this program, and deeper than we ever wanted to.

I have always used the term "compassion" to mean that I see the suffering of another and I respond. Poverty, Inc. uses that term differently. Many people in Poverty, Inc. see the suffering of another and benefit from it. These poveteers make a living from the deficiencies in a community. They study the needs, devise professions to serve them, and create institutions that are dependent upon the existence of these deficiencies. The poor are not the primary beneficiaries of Poverty, Inc. They are the raw materials. The beneficiaries are the people who make a living from Poverty, Inc.

Somehow our much-better-than-it-ought-to-be program launch had actually jammed up the unseen gears of Democratic party politics, money, and power. I still don't know what trip wires we walked through, but I do know this: For the entrenched systems, the frayed social fabric is a useful tool, and their goal is not always to repair it. If it gets repaired as a byproduct of the services they are delivering, then fine. For me, a functioning social fabric is the goal, and not the means. If we as a nation are to build our communities anew, we are going to have to walk this road too. This is the only option left for America.

OUR GENTLE NAVIGATORS

The navigators that we identified and trained in the Opportunity Community pilot project are not the only kind of navigators that there are. Three months before the Opportunity Community event happened, a local nonprofit that ran mobile medical clinics asked if they could *give me* some of their staff, their Apartment Navigators. It seems that over the years, two couples—social entrepreneurs who wanted to be navigators—had attached themselves to this organization. Both the organization and the two couples knew that they did not "fit" with each other, but until I formed the CDC, they had nowhere else to go. The idea was that the two couples would transfer over to me, and I would work with them to grow their work and impact. Thrilled, I said yes, because their organic work was right in line with what I hoped to launch through the CDC.

It was an unusually warm early-spring evening when I first met Peter and Andrea Eversmeyer at their apartment in Barberry Village. Barberry was such a lawless place that when city police responded to the constant emergency calls, they were required to roll with two backups. This created a big problem for the police, which in one year fielded 460 emergency calls. Barberry Village contains 180 apartments, meaning there was an average of two and a half calls per apartment per year. I don't know about your neighborhood, but in mine we have close to zero. On one occasion, when the police entered the compound, a gang member jumped out a second-story window onto the roof of the car to frighten them off. The yards were bare dirt, and there was an eerie quiet inside the steel fences that surrounded the hundreds of apartment units. Well, quiet except for the shouting related to domestic violence. And the gunfire. That was always loud.

A few years before, a team of young couples rented apartments and moved into Barberry to simply live their lives and be neighbors. Even though everyone on the team worked full-time, in their off time they simply hung out outside. They would arrange potlucks in the community room. They would play with kids on the filthy playground. They would be a welcoming home base for groups from outside Barberry that wanted to come in and provide relief services. Slowly, almost imperceptibly, residents of Barberry came out of their apartments and met each other. Pickup soccer games started spontaneously in the yard. The pool got cleaned up, and the manager started kicking out the worst of the hardcore criminals. The refugee resettlement agencies started placing refugees there because the rent was the cheapest in all of Portland. This team was changing the environment just by living their lives of openness and service.

The wonderful thing about having an anchor group in Barberry is that they gave outside groups a way into Barberry. If a church wanted to do an ice cream social, we could make that happen. A company did a sock drive and gathered five thousand pairs of new socks. How did they get rid of five thousand pairs of socks? They gave them to our team, who could pass out a few hundred ourselves, and we distributed the rest to a dozen other organizations in Rockwood.

Over time, a bit of funding trickled in and the team could take Iraqi kids whose families had been killed in the war on their first camping trip. Eventually the violence numbers began to move in the right direction, and after five years, the emergency calls from the area were down to 115 a year, and they're still falling.

As I got to know these social entrepreneurs, I was struck by the beauty of what they were doing. They did not have a change model, so they had no expectations of response. Simple generosity and routine neighborliness happened because these families made room in their lives and their hearts for people who had few possessions and no social capital. Over time and as money came in, I could help them with small things like paying their cell phone bills or reimbursing expenses. When they opened a Homework Club after school in the little community room, I could channel volunteers to them.

Simple generosity and routine neighborliness occurred because they made rooms in their lives and their hearts for people who had no social capital.

As word spread organically around the country that this transformative work was occurring, other couples asked about moving into Barberry or any of a number of other deeply distressed apartment complexes in Rockwood.

What struck me the most was how countercultural their work and their lives were. The church they went to didn't have an air conditioner or cushioned chairs. The music wasn't cool, and there was no screen up front for videos and song lyrics. The stage wasn't decorated. The congregation was small. But there was real community. When Dan gave a guitar lesson, or Andrea grew zucchinis, or a bunch of kids from California spent a week at Barberry on a mission trip, the activities didn't seem to amount to much. But to the people of Barberry, it was a lot. Many families there had no furniture at all, so when my team made a truck available, families could use it to retrieve donated items. Many families spoke their native language inside their apartments, so when a retiree simply read to the kids, the kids picked up English quickly.

I thought that this team was our best example of what *It's Personal*, one of our four core values, looked like. They also constantly lived out another core value, *Build Bridges, Not Armies*, because they bridged lots of outside resources to the people in the soup of Barberry Village. And when army-raisers wanted to leverage these families to gain access to Barberry Village, those army-raisers went home empty-handed, frustrated, and very critical.

From this team I learned another core value: *Reconciliation*. Reconciliation means pursuing the disconnected. It means constantly working to overcome language, culture, physical, and resource barriers to bring marginal people into the mainstream. Reconciliation means to look holistically at the disconnects people have across the five dimensions of shalom: peace with self, peace with family, peace with God, peace with community, and peace with the environment. Reconciliation means that the values of the middle- to upper-middle-class white people who surround the liminal community are not necessarily allowed to triumph over the values that the community itself holds.

This last point is not trivial. The cultural mismatch between how "we" do and how "they" do is a big one. The issue looms larger for the low-income person than it does for the upper-income person. In years past, I unknowingly brought my culture to the table in a way that reinforced the power imbalance. Now that I look back at the old me, and also at the people like me who are entering Rockwood's community in order to help, I am aghast.

Before I explain what I see when I look back, I will explain what I don't see. I don't see bad motives or arrogance. The unknowing actions and words of well-intentioned people may *appear* and *feel* to me and my neighbors as bad motives or arrogance. But I remind myself and them that we should think of these awkward interactions in the same way we think of awkward interactions with teenagers. Which is to say: tolerate a lot, encourage positive growth, and very occasionally call out the stuff that actually harms.

> **External players are part of a toxic culture that they cannot see.**

The problem is that the external players are part of a toxic culture[2] that they cannot see. People from this broader, dominant American culture can be brutal, are assuredly consumerist, and will use force if necessary to maintain their dominance. Although not one volunteer who ever came through our door consciously thought these things, almost every one of them carries a whiff of the culture that they left when they entered into our beloved community. One of the telltale signs is the emphasis on "standards." Time and time again, I disappointed my peers on the outside because my standards weren't high enough for them. "We just can't work with the Rockwood CDC," one pastor said solemnly. "Just look at your publications, with all of the typos. Your community center needs a thorough scrubbing. And this study that we're doing for the neighbors? Their attendance record is awful. Hit or miss. If they aren't showing up, then we'll have to kick them out. Our church is trying to be a source of excellence everywhere we go, and we just can't have our reputation lowered because of you."

"I get it," I said. "In your study framework, people have to be there to get all of the content. And all of the content fits together, and the class is moving on together, and you can't have people dropping in and out. Right?"

"Right."

"But in Rockwood, two-thirds commute out of the area for work because there are no jobs here. Most rely on some form of mass transit for their commute, which puts them at the mercy of the mass transit's schedule. When they get home, they face the triage that is their life—all that before they can rush to your meeting. They *want* to learn, but despite their best efforts, it's going to be hit-or-miss. Instead of expecting them to adapt to your preferred model, can you adapt your curriculum to them? They must have culturally appropriate learning modules or they're wasting their time and yours."

"Well, what does that mean, practically speaking?" she asked.

"The educational style that works best in Rockwood is called participatory learning. It starts with what people already know and builds from there. I watch in amazement when one of our teachers skilled in this practice takes a group through it. They end up teaching each other, with just a nudge from our teacher if they need more information or have somehow drawn a conclusion that is way off. It works great, and I'm never going back to PowerPoint."

When, later, I summarized this little conversation to a volunteer who actually came up from Rockwood, he said, "Sounds familiar. None of us who live in the apartments are experts about money or careers, but we *are* experts about our lives. Around here, we don't want polish. My feeling is, if it ain't rough, it ain't right."

In this booming launch of my vision for community transformation, it felt good to be in demand again. I had walked so far off my map that, when I made it back onto the map again, it was in a place I never would have imagined. In my first year in operation, I raised a paltry $58,000—but when you figure in the value of the volunteers' time and the donated goods, that figure increases to an astonishing $365,000. Friends would say to me, "See? All the struggle has been worth it," or "You must be so proud of what you've accomplished." And I was. From the day that I decided to launch, there was never a day that I didn't stand back and admire the torrent of assets that this community was unleashing for itself.

Despite that, when Lynn and I would debrief at night, both of us were deeply sad. I was fulfilled and full of purpose, but I was also full of sorrow over me and my neighbors. I would try to tell my friends, supporters, and volunteers about the existential grief inside Oregon's poorest community, but I could see that it was hard for them to relate. Many people were fascinated to take this journey with me at arm's length and to see poverty through my eyes, and they were happy to support the work, but in the end it was *my* journey— to take alone. I learned that the old word *lament* is a healing word. And so I lived an odd double-life of heartache and animation, lonely witness to a miracle: a dead community awakening to its new life.

It was now June 2013, and we had moved our headquarters into an old barber shop sitting on the land that we would redevelop. The place was pretty gritty, but it felt right to be in the soup—in the middle of the street scene that was Rockwood. While it was true that I was starting to get comfortable, I still sprang to my feet and broke out in a sweat when gunfire popped off across the street. About this time, Dre Jones-Dixon, a young African American man, lost his life in a drug deal that went bad. At the time, it seemed to me like just another stressful event. Only later would I learn how tightly my life would be interwoven with his.

CLEARING THE LAND

Sunrise Development, LLC was what we named the five-acre tract that we would redevelop. The day that Ed, the landowners, and I signed the deal, we laid plans for the demolition of the Foxy Girls strip club that dominated the site. Foxy Girls had originally been a Mexican restaurant, and it still looked like one. But it had been painted crime-scene-tape yellow, and a seven-foot-high banner that read "DANCERS," visible for three miles down the long, straight thoroughfare, had been affixed to its second story. This is where Renaldo and hundreds like him had connected to the drug trade.

When Ed and I closed the strip club, the owner made no effort to clean it up or remove her stuff. So on a Saturday morning, we walked into a place that was exactly as it had been the night before when it was full of rowdy partiers. It was horrid. This was not the type of semi-alluring place you see in cop shows on TV. It was dark and dirty, with lots of cubbies and lots of little rooms that couldn't be unlocked from the inside.

Without a word, Ed walked behind the bar and started pouring liquor down the sink. I don't know what battle he was fighting, and I never asked, but I watched him dispose of about a thousand dollars' worth of low- and high-end stuff in twenty minutes. It was thrilling. I had a rush of adrenaline, because I considered this a victory over the darkness at the heart of my neighborhood.

As I moved through the rooms and the filthy kitchen (where was the Health Department?), I discovered a back staircase that led to a second story. I wasn't prepared for what I found at the top. Any illusions of victory vanished as I walked into the room where the prostitution and human sex trafficking happened. It looked like a cross between a porn movie set and an episode of *Hoarders*. A grimy, queen-sized mattress with no sheets lay directly on the floor. Used condoms, one high-heeled shoe, a porn magazine, and needles were strewn on top of the mattress. The place stank. Around the mattress were more clothes, boxes of business records for the strip club, a closet with stacks of porn, and a countertop strewn with cigarette butts and empty liquor bottles. The window was barred, and the door that led to an outside deck was also barred. My knees got weak. I would have sat down but I couldn't imagine touching anything in that room.

Later that day, the Portland vice squad came to examine the room. The officer was also taken aback. "Usually by the time we get to a crime scene, it has been cleaned up a little," she said. "We're going to photograph all of this for training, because this is one of the few chances we get to document what these places are really like."

"I don't know how you deal with this," I said quietly. "I think I'm just going to head home now. I cannot process."

After a long pause, she said, "I think I need to go home too."

The family that had owned the land claimed that they had not known what had gone on in the upstairs room. It was the worst example of upper-middle-class "innocence" that I had encountered yet—or since. It was the second time I'd encountered the kind of evil in which simple neglect caused great unnecessary suffering. The first time was when, heading up an international poverty-fighting corporation in Manila, I held a child who was dying of nothing in particular. This time I was standing in a crime scene that had been active for years while thirty thousand cars drove by on the thoroughfare outside every single day.

The family that had owned the land weren't the only ones who could have shut down the Foxy Girls strip club. A kitchen inspection by the county health department would have closed the place, but there had been no inspections. A simple check by county officials would have revealed that this business had no permits for anything. Police presence even a few times a week would have resulted in arrests for the countless crimes committed in the parking lot every week. This shocking lack of concern for the law and for the vulnerable girls being exploited here filled me with anger.

A few weeks later, at Christmas, I sent this email to the state, metro, county, and city elected officials and staff, law enforcement, and leaders at other government agencies who directly or indirectly bore responsibility:

> I am pleased to announce that the Rockwood Community Development Corporation has permanently closed the Foxy Girls strip club. With this action, there are now no businesses left in Rockwood that are explicitly involved in the sex industry.
>
> Upon taking possession of the building, our team was able to determine that a great deal of illegal sex and drug activity had been taking place there for a long time. The Portland Police detectives who work in trafficking told me that the filth and degradation was the worst that they had ever seen.
>
> The building is cleaned out now, and will never reopen. It is slated for demolition in April, as part of Phase I of the Rockwood Sunrise development project. As we come to the end of this, our inaugural year, we are grateful to our partners in the government for their support and encouragement. Merry Christmas to you, and best wishes for the New Year.

No one wrote back.

IT'S PERSONAL

The word was spreading that things were happening in our little barbershop, and people were excited. But I was rattled. I told my friend, author William Paul Young, how I was being emotionally stripped by the ruggedness of this work. He knew a lot about rugged challenges, so I asked him if he could just tell me what I might expect in the months and years ahead.

Paul smiled. "We must do the work ourselves. We cannot ask or require of others what we are unwilling to do. The Beloved Community will be built only by authentic human beings. This requires vulnerability, empathy, and clarity. The empire that is crumbling was built on performance, production, and competition, where winning was the intended outcome. The future will be built on infinite values."

I had to process that one for a while. My personal empire in the tech world *had* been built on performance, production, and competition. But that was driven out of me, and the only path forward that I could see was to lean into my brokenness.

To give up the illusion of control and instead embrace Paul's "vulnerability, clarity, and empathy."

To approach the rest of my life with open hands and not with a clenched fist.

> **The Beloved Community will only be built by authentic human beings.**

To hold certainty at a bit of a distance and be willing to dismantle what I had built.

And what is true for me as an individual is also true for us as a Western culture that might be staring at the end of its empire. We, as a nation, like me personally, must dig into our brokenness, and we must open ourselves to a creative but vulnerable future.

So there I was, staring at the carcass of my false self and getting to know my true self, when Willie Chambers walked in the door. Willie is an African American grandfather, ex-con, and wise elder. He is a trustworthy guide to a culture that is not my own. Willie sat down to talk about things getting real, and since then he has never left.

"You heard about the murder?" I asked. "And the strip club?"

"I did," he replied wearily. "I think I can help, if you want it."

Together, Willie and I, and Kiesel and Paul and Lynn and Ed and many others, pushed forward into a new narrative of indictment ... and of hope.

CHAPTER 5

We Begin the Conversation

*T*he pilot project of creating navigation relationships worked, in the sense that we created about fifty functioning relationships. Sure, there were problems with the content and design, and there was no funding, but it seemed that these three issues could be worked out if the training company ever swallowed their disappointment and came back to the table. Despite the misfire, I was still committed to making navigation work. I knew from our work in Barberry Village that navigation and neighborliness could develop social capital in the lives of people who had almost none. So when another chance to pilot an approach came along, I was quick to jump on it. This time, the navigation approach came out of a clinical medical model.

The idea was that some of my neighbors were very expensive people for the medical system. Termed the "frequent flyers," these people had a knot of conditions—some chronic, some mental, and some that had nothing to do with medicine at all—that kept them constantly demanding medical services. And when they were in crisis (which happened a lot), these frequent flyers would dial 911 and get an ambulance ride to the emergency room. The cost to provide their care was outrageous, and ironically, the care that they were receiving was subpar because the ER is not a good place to learn how to manage conditions such as diabetes. And it is a terrible place to go to get a voucher to have your electricity turned back on.

There are a lot of frequent flyers in Rockwood.

The solution was to have the medical system pay for navigators to work with these patients in their homes, heading off that 911 call before it is placed. These navigators also work on issues broader than just the client's medical care. If a client wanted to complete her high-school diploma, then the navigator could help her enroll in a program. Or if a vaccination for the client's four-year-old was in order, then a vaccination was set up. The innovative part of this was that the navigator was paid by the medical system itself, and those funds came out of the savings in the ER. Further, the model the program followed was "pay for success," where the result was rewarded and not just the activity. For example, if a client was pregnant, the navigator would be paid a little if the client signed up for prenatal care. If the client actually went to the prenatal session, the navigator was paid more. There was payment for the client's vitamin consumption. When the baby was born full term, drug free, and healthy, the navigator was paid the most.

I loved the model, and still do. The organization that created it and got the initial funding, Project Access Now, served as the backbone or hub organization. They got some seed funding and then worked for two years to enlist forty social service agencies, health care providers, schools, and my team to implement this redesign of how services are delivered. All of these groups were to hire the navigators, recruit the families, and clear capacity in their overburdened services systems for navigator referral. With the right funding, this model could revolutionize service delivery, drive down costs, and improve outcomes. Without adequate funding, however, all that would occur is the usual fixed-pie backbiting that characterizes service delivery today.

I was on the executive steering committee with the heads of much larger organizations, so I got to see my peers up close and unfiltered. The committee's first meeting went on late into the evening, and people were tired. The hospitals and major philanthropies that had expressed enthusiasm were dropping out one by one. As the committee worked through the fine points of matching our navigation to the existing medical systems' billing codes, Emily, the CEO of one of Portland's largest services organizations, had had enough. "These codes are far too rigid and narrow," she said. "We have no staff to do this work because no one will fund us. Meanwhile, there are people out there in deep distress, and if we intake them wrong, then not only will we not be paid for serving them, but we'll be in danger of losing our funding for the entire clinic.

"I had one of our intake specialists run into my office with tears in her eyes yesterday," Emily continued. "She asked for a waiver of our normal policy so that we could see a boy who needed urgent mental health treatment. She had gone over the heads of two layers of managers to get to me. She pled her case, and I told her no. She yelled, 'Emily, if you don't approve this, that boy is going to die!'"

Emily paused, her sharp brown eyes flashing. "Well, then let him fucking die," she said. Her eyes then moistened as she felt again the pain of administrating a system that can be lethal to the most vulnerable. "And I suppose that's what he did."

I worked for years in highly competitive technology, then for a nonprofit in global relief, and now in community development, and

I had never before seen the nasty zero-sum game our collective system forces the social service agencies into. The leaders of these nonprofits are the hardest bitten executives I have ever encountered. Poverty, Inc. can make even the softest heart vile.

One feature that both the medical model and the pilot project had in common was that at their core, they were about driving efficiency into a broken system. At the end of the day, these reforms are about delivering needed relief and betterment services *for* my neighbors, and not about the development *with* my neighbors that had been and remained my goal for the CDC. In other words, in those two projects, we are doing it to our clients, and they are second-class people in the process. A paternalistic, captain-of-the-universe heart is beating at the center of many service organizations. The critique of Poverty, Inc.—that the machine fosters power imbalances and paternalism—appeared to be valid.

I was repulsed by it. I couldn't put up with the organizations' thinly veiled contempt for the very people that the leaders sought to help. And my commitment to non-hierarchical leadership was also a bad match for that approach. But then, my heart was just not in relief. Or even betterment. I had already learned that my heart was really in development. In walking with the poor. In finding the diamond-in-the-rough emerging leader who could really take her people where they all need to go. In addressing the larger, systemic issues that keep people from realizing their full potential, and then helping fix those problems so that they can rise.

All of which is, to me, the most natural thing in the world. In launching the CDC, I had made a commitment to identify the next generation of leaders and do what *they* wanted. To build on the assets that *they* possessed. To build bridges into other indigenous organizations that could work together. To get out of the "top-down" business.

I became more convinced than ever that if people are to prosper, they must do it in healthy communities, and that if communities are to heal, they must heal themselves. For them to heal themselves, the neighbors must be woven into functioning community systems where we live life together at dinner, at the library, at soccer games, at the kids' schools, regular special events, churches and associations, informal gatherings, clubs, and just running into each other in a small, walkable, downtown-like core. In the context of relationship, these neighbors would have a shared narrative of the problems of the area and an agenda for its prospering.

I was convinced that there *must* be a way to create this structure of belonging,[3] but how? Maybe the churches of the area could help, I thought. Not the churches *in* the community, but the richer churches *around* the community. I was getting a stream of calls from them as they sought to hitch a ride on my growing organization. All that I have ever done with outside requests (unless they are army-builders) is say yes. One by one, they would make their way out past the familiar Portland landmarks into hostile Rockwood territory and knock on my office door at the barbershop. We would talk for a while and then walk a few hundred feet to grab fish tacos at our neighborhood's excellent Michoacánan tacqueria. As we would sit down, I would ask the same question to everyone that I met with:

"Okay, we just walked over here from the office. How threatened do you feel right now? On a scale of 1 to 10, where 1 is you're in your backyard in a hammock on a Sunday afternoon, and 10 is 'I'm gonna die,' where are you right now?"

The average answer was seven. Seven! Seven is beyond mild alarm and into fight-or-flight territory. I could assure my guests that the walk was perfectly safe, and that I and the team worked here every day with no problems. But they were freaked out just being in this neighborhood.

I was thinking about these folks when I ran across the term *ecotourist*. The term had a mildly negative connotation, because while ecotourists think that they are earnestly engaging with the world, they are ill-equipped to do much about the problems they've learned about. I realized that many of my guests were just *emotourists*—coming into Rockwood to see poverty and meet me, but ill-equipped emotionally to do much about it.

Seven? The children in Barberry Village laugh at seven.

If the emotourists weren't much help, then I wondered whether we could build a functioning team by relying on our homeless neighbors to fulfill major roles within the CDC. Sadly, you cannot build an effective team staffed solely with deeply disabled, incarcerated, severely mentally ill, and severe drug-using people. Yes, they can build a community, sometimes quite profound, amongst themselves and their caregivers. Those at the bottom have gifts, and we encourage them to share them. We always want them at the table. But crafting a community-wide narrative and acting on it requires leadership and structure from the neighbors who at least have stable housing.

THE SOCIAL JUSTICE WARRIORS

If we can't build social fabric with the social service agencies, and the emotourists are no help, and the most distressed neighbors are not stable enough, and the systems don't want it built, then are there any options left? What about the loudest voices, the people who have a lot to say about social justice? After all, Rockwood had lots of cause-oriented people who were anxious to overturn the status quo. But the sad answer here, too, is: not so much. As the subsequent years revealed, these lone eagles are rarely equipped emotionally to be productive in a group setting. Lone eagles from academic backgrounds have a really tough time in Rockwood. Our terminology doesn't fit their buzzwords; our program doesn't conform to their specific agenda. Our approach to working together doesn't match the long list of rules governing relationships, patriarchy, and outcomes that these lone eagles frequently come armed with. We aren't Latino enough for some, and we're too rich for others. We aren't gay enough, or moderate enough, or we're too poor, or too conservative. Our privilege is showing, our progressive flag is flying, our theology needs straightening out.

My experience in a very poor community riddled with injustice is that most of the social justice warriors we've seen at work here are on a journey of their own, and they aren't able to join a larger initiative. Some are just haters. If they can't get the upper hand, then they bully or attack. Many have legitimate gripes. Some have no following, others have a huge one. Some are mentally ill. Others are sharper than anyone else in the room. It's puzzling when these people who are trying to create social change instead turn it into a "circular firing squad," trying to take out those dedicated people who share their sense of mission, but there it is. It is the campaigns of gossip and misinformation that seem to do the most damage, because in the age of social media, once the rumor is in circulation, it is everywhere. It never dies. There are former investors in my tech company who, twelve years later, circulate emails to people in my world that purport to detail the things I did wrong at that company. Why they are doing this I do not know. But I do know that none of their gossip is true.

For the first five years of building our work in Rockwood, Lynn and I would come home on a Friday night feeling bruised. I had never known this feeling before. Like a dull, aching bruise on your body, your soul and mind can also be bruised. And it was frequently these warriors for justice who bruised me the most. What saved me was that, by the time Monday morning rolled around, the bruises had healed enough to allow me back into the fight for Rockwood. Still, these injuries make it hard for me to do what I know needs to be done: acknowledging the pain that is driving the rigid thinking of these angry justice warriors, thanking them for their service, and then stepping out of the way.

Each of them eventually blasts through the community and then is gone, often leaving a wake of destruction. A big part of surviving long-term is forgiving these warriors who shoot the community's leaders in the back. Does the same thing happen in other areas of service? Yes, it's no different in church, or on school boards, or anywhere else agenda is more important than relationship. Ironic, isn't it, that their goal of creating healthy community never really gets accomplished—because they can't live in healthy community? If I could give one gift to each of these warriors, it would be this: first, be the community that you want to create.

First, be the community that you want to create.

The social justice warriors, while the loudest voices in the room, are also sometimes the ones who understand the nature of poverty the least. Globally, the efforts to encourage human flourishing are creative and confident. Global poverty is on the run, and it is not by accident. The industry knows how to alleviate poverty and has precise ways of applying the accumulated decades of insight and practice. In the Philippines, the percentage of people in poverty has dropped fast. Today only about 15 percent of the country is below the poverty line, the same as the US.

The optimism of international poverty-alleviation efforts stands in stark contrast to the pessimism of our domestic fight. Sour justice warriors and defeatist politicians of the type common in America simply are nowhere to be seen when you are on the ground in countries like the Philippines that are rapidly advancing in the fight against poverty. In that country, there is a national sense—visible in the media, overheard at cocktail parties, experienced by the poor themselves—that the elimination of unnecessary human suffering is occurring right before their eyes. Their economy is growing twice as fast as ours, and the poor are disproportionally benefitting from this immense change. They are proud of this national accomplishment and are puzzled that a similar ethos is not evident everywhere. I wonder if someday the US can regain this attitude of "can-do" and alleviate our unnecessary suffering.

Over the years we've worked in Rockwood, I've had to learn to rise above criticism and stay above it by focusing on the least person in the community and what they need, who they are, and what they bring to the table. This approach is disruptive to the agendas of myself and others, and one evening I was grousing about this to my board member Laura Bolanos-Ramirez, who grew up in Rockwood. She is the daughter of Mexican immigrants who came to the US for a better way of life and has lived in the same apartment complex her entire life, surrounded by the same forty families. She is the only person in the entire complex who went to college. "Laura, I've tried the social justice warrior route, and that's no good for us. I've tried the navigation route, and it's a good solution, but incomplete. What am I missing here? I mean, where are the neighbors in this? Who knows who the people are and what they want?"

"Nobody knows us, Brad. None of the outside organizations or the city or the churches knows who I am—or *mi familia*. It was so hard growing up here. I wanted to organize my people, but there was no support. I wanted to help kids get to college, but that was unattainable for so many reasons. If there had been a Rockwood CDC when I was growing up, this whole community would have been prosperous."

LET THE CONVERSATION BEGIN

When we began, I was struck by just how isolated people are in Rockwood, and I didn't know what to do about it. So I reached back out to Dr. Loren Sickles to see what he thought about creating a holistic structure of belonging. "That's an easy one," he said. "You begin with food and community conversations. You build from there. That's the only way to weave a fabric where none exists."

Loren explained that the practice of holding community conversations is a well-established element of an Asset Based Community development approach. There are more than eighty different engagement models being used in the US alone, and the leading group that tracks them and propagates them is the National Coalition for Dialog and Deliberation. Some of the terms and models out there are *World Café*, *Slow Democracy*, *Appreciative Inquiry*, and just about anything with the word *participatory* in it. Each has its own design details that make it better or worse suited for specific community contexts, and successful practitioners put in a lot of thought before they pick a specific framework. All of them share principles of welcoming, listening, analyzing, reporting, and acting. Each has the same elements of a convening space, a facilitator, food, translation, white boards, interactive discussions, and carefully worded questions. They do not have predetermined outcomes, and the neighbors decide for themselves what, if anything, happens next.

None of the models are quite like the similar-sounding term *community organizing*, which you frequently hear in politics. Community organizing is often about creating an army that wields power to achieve a specific agenda item. It might be a useful tool for the neighborhood to occasionally use if it must power its way through a particular systemic barrier that is impeding its progress. But it cannot be the main tool because it frequently leads to abuse. Communities find themselves manipulated by skilled organizers who simply see the community as a tool for their agenda. Thus, Poverty, Inc. finds yet one more expression of itself. For Poverty, Inc., the poor are not the beneficiaries. The poor are the raw materials. The beneficiaries are the people who run Poverty, Inc.

Loren helped us clarify what we wanted to do—and what we did not want to do. My team set out to design a specific set of practices. We adopted a disciplined and rigorous approach to data collection, analysis, and dissemination. The emphasis is on fidelity to the process, and not on outcomes. The timeframe is forever. We branded the facilitated conversations Rockwood Speaks! and began with a three-tiered framework:

Level	Focus
1	Connect
2	Act
3	Act for Change

Level One is about *connecting* neighbors, so that they meet each other, learn about issues, and improve democratic attitudes and skills. They learn who lives where, who is related to whom, what their shared concerns are, and what community assets exist. This connecting is done through meetings that run about ninety minutes and are held at different times of the day and week. These initial conversations are limited to twenty people and conducted as small table discussions with four to five people per table. If most participants in the conversation are non-English speakers, as is common in Rockwood, then translation is provided and the English speakers wear the headphones, and not the other way around. Table discussions revolve around a series of questions that explore in broad terms our neighbors' beliefs and understanding of the Rockwood community. Each table is covered in thick white butcher paper, on which a recorder captures the core points of each table member as they discuss the prescribed questions.

These meetings begin with an ice-breaker that uses a six-foot-by-four-foot map of Rockwood. Everyone gets three sticky dots. They use the yellow one to identify where they live. They use the red one to show where they feel unsafe. And the green one marks where they have positive experiences. When everyone has placed their dots, we ask some questions:

- Looking at the dots on the map, what impresses you?
- What changes have you seen in Rockwood that contribute to a positive or negative neighborhood experience?
- If you had the time and resources, how would you confront some of Rockwood's challenges?
- What supports would you need to address the challenges you face?
- What are priority topics for you?

One warm evening, we convened a group of Tongan residents. Because we had a little bit of funding from the county for our work, we'd been able to produce a publicity flyer for the meeting, in Tongan and featuring the county's logo. During the meeting, one of the Tongan moms said that when she received the flyer the week before, she framed it and put it on the wall in her apartment. Our facilitator asked her why. "When you know the history of my people," she said, "you will understand. That there is a meeting where people want to know what I think, and that the flyer is in Tongan, and on the same piece of paper is a logo from the government is really special. To be honest, this blows my mind." That is the voice of displacement.

I am often asked why my organization is the trusted convener when the government should be doing these sessions. When a government employee convenes a meeting, the conversation changes. And this has nothing to do with someone's skills in conducting a dialog. It has to do with a business card. We all view government as the solution, so the conversation inevitably shifts to problems. But creating a community is not initially about problem-solving. It is focused on possibilities and new narratives. If government wants these conversations to happen and to be successful, then they should pay for a community-based organization to convene them. Once we started these conversations, so many workers, government and otherwise, wanted to be a "fly on the wall" that there would have been more flies than neighbors. So we didn't allow anyone to be present in the room who was not actively participating, and the only participants were neighbors.

Over the years, my team has engaged over four thousand adults in these facilitated conversations. We have done them in English, Russian, Rohingya, Spanish, Tongan, Swahili, Dinka, Arabic, and Chuukese. We have hired and trained eight cultural liaisons who can conduct outreach in culturally specific ways. All of the content from these sessions is transcribed into a rigorous spreadsheet that evaluates and aggregates the conversation and compares the results across cultural barriers. From this, we produce written reports, available to download for free on our website.

People from groups that we have never even heard of tell us all the time that they used this previously unknown data to fund and create new community assets. For example, an aging church was closing its doors and turning the building over to their denomination. The denomination used Rockwood Speaks! data to determine that people in the area needed space to meet, so they wrote a successful grant application to turn the mothballed building into a vibrant new arts and culture space that today is completely full. A developer used the data to understand the cultural diversity needs of a major new housing complex he was building. The health clinic across the street from the governor in the capital, the county human services department, the city managers who would never set foot in Rockwood, churches, foundations, and plain old neighbors all were hungry to use this data to peer inside the window that we opened into this opaque place.

From these hundreds of Level One (*connect*) conversations, we developed the second tier of the three-tier framework. Level Two (*act*) conversations convene people from Level One who want to focus on a specific area. Level Two people know that together they can achieve more. A simple Level Two conversation convened the Latino residents of an apartment with their manager to explain how they wanted the exterior lights to be rearranged. They believed that they could create a safer space, and in the end the apartment manager agreed and made the changes. Other Level Two conversations have helped the EPA in organizing the cleanup of a toxic site, addressed the injustice of police actions toward African Americans, and planned a block party.

From these scores of Level Two conversations, we developed the third tier of the three-tier framework. Level Three (*change*) conversations convene people from Levels One and Two who want to commit to systemic change. Systemic change occurs when neighbors spur both individual and collective action, improve institutional decision-making, and increase civic capacity. At Level Three, leaders have organized into steering teams, and my staff supports and encourages their work. Our goal is to spin them out completely so that they are self-sustaining and self-replicating. For example, our Homework Club at Barberry Village developed its own leadership, volunteers, and funding, and we released them to run their own thing. Many people who volunteer on my Level Three initiatives do not even realize that my team created the initiative in the first place, and that suits me just fine. I was amused when I asked one of the Level Three leaders if her huge action team would appreciate receiving individual thank-you notes. She smiled and said, "I think that they would be confused why Brad Ketch even knew who they were, much less thanked them." Perfect. The community gains new life, and my fingerprints are never found.

Another Level Three group was Business Speaks!. This large team worked on the systemic changes that entrepreneurs and small businesses need. They forged import/export channels, sponsored seminars on business skills, sought out new capital sources, and guided the creation of the Sunrise Center Kitchen.

We have other Level Three groups that focus on food systems, community resources, capital formation, and community health. Not every Level Three group is a success. Some have disbanded when they encountered too much systemic resistance around a legal center, housing, or immigration.

Perhaps the most vigorous Level Three effort has been the Shalom Rockwood Network. Although the Rockwood CDC is not a religious organization, a holistic approach to community requires means to encourage peace with God. Many of us in Rockwood have a deep and vibrant personal Christian faith; others have no faith at all; and still others are Muslim, Jewish, or committed to other faith systems. Believing that our diversity is our strength, we convened Shalom Rockwood as a multi-faith network, but we soon found out that Rockwood has no organized faith communities that are *not* Christian. So Shalom Rockwood has taken a distinctly Christian identity and will almost surely stay that way. Should other faith communities emerge, then we will work through the Level One → Level Two → Level Three process to engage those communities and integrate them into the Shalom Network when they want to be.

The scope of the Shalom Rockwood Network is breathtaking, and it has been celebrated worldwide. Pastors lead congregations in English, Romanian, Spanish, Arabic, and Russian. Just about every ethnic or racial identity that occurs in Rockwood has a home. One church-growth expert recently remarked that this was the most diverse and healthiest network of leaders that he has ever encountered anywhere in the US. About forty-three churches or nonprofit groups attend the twice-yearly network gathering where they work on shared social impact. They meet to pray and worship together so that they can grow their unity and interdependence. Most summers they hit the streets with "Prayers and Tamales," and *thousands* of our neighbors are cared for in one way or another. The steering team for the Shalom Rockwood Network is the most multi-cultural and authentic group found in any sector of the community, and it is very satisfying for me personally to now collaborate as equals with these men and women who are also deeply committed to shalom.

We had finally hit on our way to create the structure of belonging. Navigators alone could not create it, emotourists could not create it, and social justice warriors could not create it. Only the neighbors themselves can take the neighborhood where it needs to go.

This sudden explosion of speaking where before there was only silence got a lot of attention from every sector—except for the city of Gresham, where the Rockwood neighborhood is situated. I was concerned that all of this passion at street level might not work its way up to the systems level naturally, so we created a companion initiative called Rockwood Listens. Rockwood Listens is an event that occurs just one night every couple of years and connects the qualitative and quantitative data, plus the neighbors who generated it, to the leaders of the various systems (governmental, health, education, faith, business, and neighborhood) who can make decisions about the allocation of resources. Since this was an event that had never happened before, we put a huge effort into personally inviting everyone and hoping for the best.

The night finally came, and people started to arrive. This was before I and others had developed new places to assemble, so we crammed into a little school cafeteria. What a fun evening, as newly engaged neighbors saw their comments fed back to them. The

Ixtapans had no idea that the Somalis had problems with the bus system just like they did. The Pentecostal church pastor learned that a new jobs-training program that could benefit his congregation of manual laborers was getting off the ground. For the first time, the county and state leaders met the beleaguered renters who just wanted a shot at home ownership.

The only local body that Rockwood Listens did not impact was the city of Gresham, because no one came. I thought it odd that the mayor and city councilors would blow off this inaugural event, but I later learned that that was intentional.

The food was fantastic at this event, of course, because my neighborhood is a buffet of cultural cuisine. The county hired an artist to commemorate the event. She taped twenty feet of white rolled paper to the wall in the cafeteria and created a cartoon infographic of the discussion. Here is just one of the panels. And she did it in real time! Amazing.

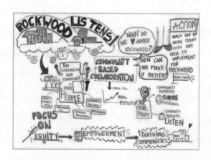

Our efforts to weave the fabric of social capital were working. It took intense focus and a little bit of funding, and now three thousand people have joined in the conversation. Hundreds have engaged further than that first conversation. Individuals whose first exposure ever to civic discourse are now leaders. Some have run for office and won. Many are on our Level Two and Level Three leadership teams. Others are now part of partner organizations and are helping those organizations drive results.

As long as we can keep starting Level One conversations and stay true to our role as an impartial and transparent convener, then I am hopeful for Rockwood. Our experience with Rockwood Speaks! taught us our fourth and final core value: Never Leave the Table. That means that no matter how high or how low the community goes, and no matter how excited or discouraged we are, we will always be here. It means that my emotional state cannot be governed by outcomes, but instead by process. The measure of success for me is the number of people engaged or the quality of that engagement, and not the tangible change in the community.

People frequently ask me what outcome I want for Rockwood. I happily tell them that I do not know, because my community has not discovered its shared outcome in its entirety even yet. This value speaks of fidelity to the process: keeping the rules of engagement regardless of outcome, always asking who is not at the table who should be, holding the heads of the systems accountable for the human suffering they have caused or allowed, instilling hope in the hopeless, and releasing leaders to build on our initiatives without us. Fidelity to the process does not mean that we are rigid, because after all, we have to adapt it to around a hundred cultures. But it does mean being intentional, because our processes keep us at the table even during those inevitable times when our passion is at a low point. Because of process, not every option is open anymore. But also because of process, the option to stay engaged for the long term *is* open.

I am a better man because of the friends I have made with my neighbors who have now learned to speak—through Rockwood Speaks! The voices that I hear tell me that the twilight of the old and the dawn of the new in America is nothing to be afraid of.

And those voices come from my neighbors.

CHAPTER 6

Let a Hundred Flowers Bloom

The Rockwood Community Development Corporation took off with a boom, and hundreds—then thousands—of people got involved. Folks would say, "I've never seen anything like this." Our revenues grew quickly, although never quickly enough to dig Lynn and me out of the hole that we had dug for ourselves by starting a nonprofit in the depth of the Great Recession. The CDC's cash revenues hit $100,000, then $200,000, but it was never enough. Even as we were giving birth to a large-scale community revitalization, our heat was turned off once at home, and there would be no health insurance for years. I'd begun with an unspoken expectation that if I sacrificed, others would respect that and respond with their own gifts. And that certainly happened a lot and continues to this day. But others wanted to take advantage of our sacrifice and move in to control what we had created. Eventually, they realized that there was nothing to gain because there were no real resources holding us up. People assume that, because the CDC is thriving, someone is writing big checks behind the scenes, and that if they get close enough, they can see the man behind the curtain. Then they find out that there is no curtain, no magic checkbook, and they leave. Few people outside my board knew that the sacrifices we had made to get the RCDC started continued, equally acute, into its fifth and even sixth year.

Dying to myself, it turned out, is not a one-time event. It is Every. Single. Day.

Despite my success at raising and deploying volunteer resources, I also needed cash, and that resource was always scarce. I was surprised that, several years into the creation of the CDC, I was still having trouble nurturing donors. I had always been a good fund-raiser for my tech and nonprofit projects. I knew big money and big philanthropy well, having leveraged them in my previous position as CEO of a large multinational relief and development agency, so I had assumed that I would be able to bring huge new resources to this forgotten part of the world.

I had also thought that, because community building is not expensive, and because it is slow, I would be able to find and keep lots of donors who would be committed to the overall vision for the long haul and who would be asked to give only $100/month. It also was a good theory. But it hasn't turned out that way. Foundations have been either completely dismissive or so slow to understand holistic community development that they are only now coming around, years into our presence here. Government grants tend to go to organizations that are providing relief services, and rich regional churches refuse to respond to the needs in their own backyards.

One evening I was presenting the concept of Relief → Betterment → Development to the board of a big area church. One of the elders interrupted me. "Let me understand this. He turned to the pastor. "Why is it that every dollar we spend overseas is for development, and every dollar we spend domestically is for relief? Why is that?" The pastor didn't have a good answer.

Individual donors have had a very different profile than I imagined. Instead of low and slow, our gifts have come from people who will write a single check in the $5,000 to $25,000 range, and then not give again for two or three years. As time went on, finding and retaining donors became less of a problem because earned income from our community center and from our investments eventually made us sustainable. But getting to that point was a long and hard journey for us and for similar organizations we know. In the US, community development efforts need reliable sources of public or private funding.

If it felt as if I was hewing donors from granite, what was not difficult was the explosion of creativity that came up from the neighborhood and our partners. Kept down and kept out for so long, they emerged out of nowhere, highly motivated to forge solutions for their people. By then we had outgrown the barbershop and moved into a little red house around the corner. The barbershop was then demolished to make way for my future Sunrise Development mega-project. In fact, the house we moved into was also on the site of the new development and was scheduled for demolition in eighteen months.

I converted the garage of our new "red house" office into a conference room where we held our bi-monthly Lunch and Learn meetings—ninety-minute sessions open to anyone who wanted to drop in and bring a sack lunch. We covered three topics:

- This Is Rockwood
- Principles of Community Development
- This Is the Rockwood CDC

Hundreds of people have participated in a Lunch and Learn, and dozens of initiatives, programs, and policy changes trace their genesis to the newbies who sat around this table, engaging in Rockwood for the very first time.

One Thursday at our regular Lunch and Learn, a tall, good-looking, young African American and his wife joined us and other neighbors at the table. When it came time for Vince Jones-Dixon to introduce himself, he said, "I'm not from Rockwood, but I want to know how I can make a difference. Three years ago my brother was shot here in a drug deal that went bad, and—"

"Vince!" I said. "I was just across the street when that happened. It was a warm June afternoon, and my door was open. I heard the pops. That was your brother?"

Vince and I knew immediately that our paths were linked. For the next two hours he absorbed everything we could tell him about our community and how to transform it. Vince committed to being ready any time we needed him. Neither of us would have guessed that Vince's journey would take him into the heart of racism in Gresham and finally to a seat on the city council.

The living room and kitchen of the house held a smaller conference table and a computer for the use of interns or volunteers. It turned out to be a great benefit to local social entrepreneurs just to have a free computer and printer that they could drop in and use.

One bedroom in our new building served as the office for a volunteer who was paid by a partner organization that created the Rockwood English Language Institute (RELI). This linguist with international development experience was aghast when he learned that Oregon's most diverse community did not have English language classes. Such courses are commonly available at community colleges, but there were no such colleges anywhere near Rockwood. To make matters worse, many of Rockwood's most vulnerable residents were illiterate not just in English, but in their own language too. Most English as a Second Language programs start with the literacy that the adult already possesses in his own language and builds from there. RELI starts from scratch. And it is still going strong.

The same room serves as the office for my wife and co-founder, Lynn, who spearheaded all of our community health efforts, as well as navigator activities, Rockwood Speaks!, Rockwood Listens, the Shalom Rockwood Network, and the Rockwood Community Action Team (a network of ninety community advocates and service providers). Lynn had also created a program to get Rockwood's thirty-nine corner stores to carry fresh fruits and vegetables. And if all of that weren't enough, she trained community health workers, hosted renters' rights workshops, and carried her weight in planning Rock the Block, the annual summer party for three thousand of our closest friends.

Lynn also worked to create and launch the Interconnecting Your Community seminar, which targets adults who are leading multicultural teams. We initially created it to help two faith communities, who were considering merging, to identify and overcome their cultural differences. One group, the Americans, didn't know that they had a culture until they were in proximity to a different one. The other church was Latino, and they put family, consensus, community, and harmony first. The two bodies needed our seminar in order to create a new church culture that worked for all. Another example: Russians and Mexicans rub shoulders in Rockwood all the time. Russians value strict child discipline, and the Mexicans value loose child discipline. Both parenting styles result in adults who are equally successful, so there is no ultimate better or worse. But when you've got Russians at the same event as Mexicans and the Mexican kids are zooming around while the Russian kids are sitting there maintaining order, the Russians are about to head for the exits. Our seminar helps in mutual understanding and accommodation.

Any time I could, I would commit my resources to serving as a backbone organization—a hub. That can feel sort of grab-baggy, with a dizzying array of apparently dissimilar activities. But if an organization is committed to holistic transformation, then health, business, faith, education, housing, justice, and neighborliness will all be firing at the same time.

As a hub, we created and hosted the first candidate forums that Rockwood had ever had so that our neighbors could be engaged in upcoming elections. We tapped newly woke Vince Jones-Dixon to host this candidate forum, and he was invigorated by the experience.

We frequently lead the collective action of all of East County's leaders in addressing systemic issues. When a state-level child care agency announced that they were pulling out of East County, we led the coalition that called them to accountability and got that decision partially reversed. We work to create broad policy and system changes.

To finish the tour of the red house office: Sitting next to Lynn is our bookkeeper. And in the next office down the hall, me. The reason I chose this room and positioned my little desk against the easterly facing window is because from here I could look directly across the street into the apartment row that Renaldo had lived in. He and his family were long gone by the time we moved our offices here, but every day I was reminded of him. If I was feeling particularly smug about our accomplishments, all I had to do was glance up from my desktop and flash back to that day seven years before when poverty invaded my world.

ROCKWOOD KNOCKS

Sharing my office was our volunteer who runs Rockwood Knocks—an annual event run by the CDC. Like Speaks!, Knocks was all about gathering in-depth data from our community. But unlike the qualitative data generated by Speaks!, Knocks was all about quantitative data collection. I had to go out and collect my own in-depth data about my neighbors because there was no available pool of data. I am glad that I did, because the data we gathered over time gave us insights into the area no one had possessed before. For example, before Knocks, no one knew that half of Rockwood residents get their groceries at the gas station. Another example: Seven hundred Rockwood families could afford better apartments if someone built them. What I learn about our specific plot of dirt through Rockwood Knocks is frequently contrary to the usual narrative of what a low-income community needs. Once I learn these things and share this reality with others, solution sets start to become apparent very quickly.

To gather this data, I needed a battalion of data gatherers. I can't afford to pay people to do this work, nor could any other organization in our area. That being true—how did Rockwood Knocks get started?

One day I received a call from the leader of a Christian organization called Cru. They hold a raucous annual three-day conference for college students in Portland, attended by about six hundred kids. Their conference format calls for all six hundred kids to hit the streets for an afternoon to reach out to Portlanders. The leader who called me wondered if I could put six hundred kids to work in Rockwood. I was floored. Putting six hundred people to work is nearly impossible. Although every family in Rockwood has almost overwhelming need, there is no way to get granular enough to meet those needs on just one afternoon per year—with strangers, no less. But in a flash, I envisioned how Knocks could work. I saw two or three hundred teams of a couple of students each, knocking on every door in Rockwood. They could drop off flyers from all of the social service agencies, telling people how to access services. They could pick up garbage. They could distribute voter registration packets. And they could ask our survey questions. Plus, because their organizational focus is primarily spiritual, their kids could engage my neighbors in spiritual conversations—only if the neighbor wished.

I usually work collaboratively with my teammates, and I'm hesitant to commit my organization's resources unless all of us are on board. But this time the opportunity seemed so incredible—as well as overwhelming—that when I gathered my team to discuss it, I started with words I almost never say: "Trust me." Then I dove into a description of my vision, which all of us knew would be a logistical nightmare. Even though the people on my team thought that I had lost my mind, I told the leader at Cru, "Yes, indeed, we can use six hundred kids for an afternoon." I gathered a small team of volunteers who had said that they were available for "whatever" and communicated my vision to them. They, too, all looked at me as if I was nuts, because they had absolutely no idea how this could come together.

But it did.

Jacqui mentioned the project to a friend at church the next Sunday and walked away with a check for $3,000 to cover the cash costs.

Wayne, a regional manager for 7-Eleven, produced six hundred vouchers for a free hot dog and soda at any of the four 7-Elevens in the neighborhood. He was glad to get rid of the franks because they were set to expire five days after our event!

TriMet, the light rail system in Portland, agreed to add extra train cars to get the kids from the event hotel out to Rockwood. Each social service agency dropped five thousand flyers off in the garage of my office. Boy Scouts showed up and stuffed tens of thousands of flyers into thousands of bags. Others called apartment managers and received permission to enter the properties. A film crew volunteered to shoot, and a nonprofit group gave us an event headquarters for free. A local nonprofit that worked on environmental cleanup donated a dumpster and six hundred garbage bags.

Neighborhood captains offered to troubleshoot if problems arose in Oregon's most violent neighborhood. A friendly geek volunteered to program Survey Monkey so that thousands of survey results could tabulate in real time from the kids' smartphones. When a stuck community begins to get unstuck, the release of resources is magical.

The afternoon finally came for the first Rockwood Knocks. No one really knew what to expect. It was December 30, 2013, and in Portland that can mean anything from 70 degrees to pounding rain to a sheet of ice on the rail tracks. But the day was dry and warm. The streets were calm, and there were no violent incidents. It went off like clockwork, and in just three hours on the streets about eight hundred valid surveys were collected, a dumpster was overflowing with garbage gathered from the now-much-cleaner streets and side-walks, thousands of people had a voting packet and information on services in their hands, and hundreds of Cru people had prayed with my neighbors. Some of those spiritual encounters had been dramatic. Our Salesforce CRM (customer relation-ship management) database bulged with 160 new neighbor volunteers. Every college student had been personally impacted by his direct face-to-face with immigrants, refugees, and intergenera-tional white poor people he had never imagined would be a part of his conference experience.

When a stuck community begins to get unstuck, the release of resources is magical.

The Cru leadership was ecstatic. "In all of the other city confer-ences around the US, we just fan out and hit the streets to pray with people. While that is fine, most of the kids just end up wandering around, so for most of them it's kind of a wasted part of our confer-ence. But here in Rockwood, we had more impact on more people and in more aspects of their lives than we've ever even heard of!" Cru voluntarily took up a collection from these college kids, and ended up giving the Rockwood CDC $13,000 with no strings attached for our work in Rockwood. When the next year rolled around, Cru wanted to do it again. And then a third year. And then a fourth year. Cru has produced videos about Rockwood Knocks that have been viewed around the world.

The end result of this survey data was a robust longitudinal study of our neighborhood. From a statistician's perspective, much of the data was not particularly "clean," and is thus invalid, but our purpose has never been academic. We are practitioners, and "good enough" is good enough. The data also tightly correlated to the qualitative data that we collected in Rockwood Speaks!, and there was no gap or confusion between the two different data methods. Thus, we had gained enough knowledge to be able to clearly and forcefully advocate for policy changes based on actual data, and not just on anecdotes. This data is on our website and has gone into foundation requests. It found its way into government analysis, from the governor's office on down. It has informed decisions about how health care systems would allocate scarce resources.

I believe that the most profound impact of Rockwood Knocks was unspoken and unmeasurable. People in Rockwood are not used to having their opinions sought out. In Rockwood, simply posing questions and then being willing to listen to the answers is a powerful act. It opens windows in people's minds that eventually result in outcomes that are completely unforeseen. Recently, for instance, a local political action group was successfully launched in Rockwood, and their leader was elected to Gresham's city council. While the Rockwood CDC made little direct contribution to getting him on the council, for four years we distributed through Rockwood Knocks five thousand voter registration packets annually. We also conducted the first candidate forum that Rockwood had ever seen, and we engaged over 2,500 adults in facilitated conversations. We think those actions had an impact: When the right candidate came along with the right organizing strategy, the match he lit touched kindling that was already soaked in gas because of our efforts.

SEEING THE FOREST THROUGH THE TREES

After four or five years of frenetic activity, I often wondered how all of our efforts in Rockwood were adding up. How do I measure shalom across its five aspects: self, family, community, God, and environment? Should I point to the Peace Award bestowed on Lynn and me by an ecumenical organization? Should I just reckon that if the budget was growing, then we were doing something right?

In the end, I stopped focusing on outcomes entirely. My role in Rockwood was to occupy this space until others in the neighborhood were ready to move into it. I held it with open hands, trying my best to be attentive to and responsive to the voice of the community. Eventually I stopped thinking the way I had been taught while studying for an MBA. Rather than looking for efficiency and effectiveness, I began to look for life. Some of my teammates were indeed efficient and effective, but after a couple of years, there was no observable life emerging from their efforts. Others appeared to lack any structure or clarity in their areas, and yet life was springing up everywhere around them. What accounted for that difference? The people whose work generated life were more relational and strategic, and less task oriented and check-box driven.

It's not that success relies on extroverts able to network with each other, because some of our life-givers are introverts. But it is true that success relies on gentleness, transparency, vulnerability, and hopefulness. The life-givers are happy when their fruit grows on other people's trees; they don't feel the need to claim credit.

I eventually also learned that the opposite of efficiency is not inefficiency. It is resilience. In the declining world of relief and humanitarian aid, efficiency is the dominant cultural value. In the rising world of development, resilience is the dominant cultural value. A resilient community:

- has many voices at the table who each present their own realities;
- goes slowly as it builds action from a base of healthy relationships;
- values long-term sustainability over short-term gain; and
- lives in the tension of differing agendas by staying engaged and being okay without immediate resolution.

As my work in the neighborhood grew and matured, I regularly checked in with Dr. Andrew Marin. The UN has accredited Andy as a mediator in ninety-six countries; thus, he is considered one of the foremost global experts on conflict analysis, mitigation, and resolution. His work spans the corporate and government sectors on five continents—from stabilizing social and organizational conflict levels in Fortune 500 companies to leading a team in ISIS-occupied Iraq on behalf of a multi-government conflict management initiative. This diverse portfolio has led the BBC to recently call Dr. Marin's work "a hopeful model for the future." Previously, for thirteen years, he was the founder and president of a nonprofit widely credited with creating a new cultural category of building bridges between the LGBTQ community and conservatives in social, political, and religious contexts. He additionally served for five years as an advisor to the Obama White House on conflict resolution and social change. Really, the four core values for the Rockwood CDC were derived from his book *Our Last Option*.

The opposite of efficiency is not inefficiency. It is resilience.

When Andy asked me how we had adapted his values to our work, I said, "Our first core value is to build bridges, not armies. In humility, we invite all people of goodwill to the community table.

Secondly, for us, it's personal. This is our community, and our role is to be present, bear witness to injustice, and call others into our third value, reconciliation. That's much easier said than done, which is why our fourth value is never leave the table. We are far from perfect and have more missed opportunities and failures than wins, but we have persevered in our calling."

"That's really good to hear, Brad," Andy said. "Those core values form a framework of commitment. What is our value? Reconciliation. How do we do that? We live in the tension. How do we live in the tension? We stay at the table. How do we stay at the table? Through faithfulness. It's not necessarily a step-by-step. If I am faithful in this community, faithful to seeing it through, then because of that extreme commitment, regardless of whatever roadblocks are thrown in the way, over time we will be successful. I succeed because I am faithful. And that success is measured in social change for good. All of these things are intertwined, such that if you base your understanding on reconciliation, then it's just a matter of time until change happens. It could take one year, or it could take ten years.

"I succeed because I am faithful. The success is social change for good.

"So that's why today, in my government and social change work, in particular, it's not about trying to revalidate the principles. They've already been validated. They're already in place. And they work in a variety of contexts, from my experiences in Boystown all the way to Iraq."

NO GOOD DEED GOES UNPUNISHED

As the impact of the Rockwood CDC grew, the Sunrise Development project was also moving along. All of the original buildings that had made up the two-acre Disneyland of human depravity were demolished except for the little red house that was now our office. We wanted to use our five-acre campus to replicate the success of the East Lake neighborhood in Atlanta. There, they put a quality public charter school in the center and then built multi-income housing around it.

Just a few miles away from Rockwood was the Corbett Charter School, which was getting headlines for its incredible quality. The headmaster of that school had always wanted to move into the heart of Rockwood and bring their fantastic quality to 730 low-income children, primarily of color, for free. The Corbett school was willing to sign a long-term lease that would allow us to get the building financed. And with the anchor firmly established, the financing of the remaining three buildings on the site would be easy…or at least that was the theory.

I built a financial model for the school based on their operating history. I showed it to my partner, Ed, who said that the finances were "disturbing but doable"—a phrase I recalled many times in the subsequent years as I worked to get other projects done in Oregon's poorest community. Ed and I both believed that the risk was worth it, and he began writing checks to pay for some of my time, the land development, and the architect.

Getting the banks behind the project turned out to be hard— much more so than I had expected, given that the cash flow from the school is backed by the State of Oregon. This is the reality of investing in an underinvested community.

Eventually, there remained only one hurdle to clear in order to begin work on this cornerstone of our strategy: We needed the local public school system, the Reynolds School District, to agree to allow the charter school to operate within their borders. But Oregon's teachers' union has a lock on the public school system, and they didn't want it. My Rockwood CDC team mobilized local people, especially Latino parents, and together we all confidently made our way to the school board meeting—where I was truly shocked to hear the board reject the proposal, despite the voices of the Rockwood neighbors at the meeting. (Sadly, that caused many of our Latino parents to permanently disengage from civic life.) At the meeting, the board members lied about what our headmaster had written in his application, and they refused to answer direct questions. They ended up ignoring state law, and pleasing the teachers' union in the process. The headmaster was so discouraged that he eventually moved away from Oregon, a great loss to our beleaguered state with too many horrible schools.

I walked away from that expensive debacle thinking, Why bother going to the existing dysfunctional leadership and asking permission to transform the community if I'm just going to be told no? I realized that I would have to fight a lot harder than I would have previously thought prudent or just.

What we were doing in building "up" from the streets was amazing—but the system at the top was not responding, and our Rockwood neighbors were starting to get frustrated. I had begun this effort in the belief that the systems are unresponsive simply because no one had yet presented them with an alternative way of being that they could say yes to. I had believed that if I proposed an appealing model—and never left the table—the systems would gladly come along. Others in our circle—the more radical social justice warriors— had a far more damning critique of the unresponsive power brokers at the top. I had always thought that damning critique to be wrong. Now, though, I was growing increasingly doubtful that the leaders in Gresham and the Reynolds School District and the other systems standing in our way were showing all of their cards. I was starting to see examples of what I could only call intentionality around the injustices of Rockwood. I had begun with the belief that the cold and callous poveteers were the exception. Now I began to wonder: Were there more of them than I'd thought?

I checked with Dr. Marin once again to see what had happened when his community-building project in Boystown (the Chicago neighborhood) encountered resistance.

"Andy," I said, "back in the days of Communist China, Mao announced that public engagement would be encouraged from then on. He wanted new ideas, and he wanted people to become leaders. He said, 'Let a hundred flowers bloom.' So everyone responded. And then the next year he revealed that the purpose of the 'hundred flowers' campaign had simply been to find the dissidents. He now knew who his enemies were. Sometimes I worry that all of the flowers blooming in Rockwood might meet with a nasty backlash. I even heard from a friend of the Gresham mayor's that he'd said, 'If Brad thinks that he is improving anyone's life, he is completely delusional.'"

"Right!" Andy agreed. "In my experience, when I would tell the politicians what was going on, they would literally laugh out loud in my face and say, 'That's impossible.' Each time I heard that, I would say, 'You can't tell me it's impossible, because it's already happening.' And they would send me on my way. Person after person. From the mayor's office all the way down to a local store owner or pastor. I kept saying, 'Just come and see. It's happening.' But none of these people with 'titles' would come. If I managed to get one meeting with them, then when I tried to set up another, I found that they weren't willing to give it more time. The door was shut. I had always thought of Chicago as a very leftward-leaning city. Democratic mayors, aldermen, and senators. One would think, just based on perception, that in doing this kind of work with the LGBTQ community, the Democrat-based government would be on board. Instead, they objected to my work not because it was about the LGBTQ community, but because we were working to build bridges between them and the conservatives, and you can't have a bridge with only one side. Both sides need to be actively engaged and involved. The liberals were horrified that I was even trying to include people from the right—whether politically, socially, or religiously. I had to acknowledge that nobody of influence was going to help us, not even a tiny bit.

"I was young, and I was starting this from nothing. I thought if I could get just one person of influence from the city to vouch for us, it would carry a lot of weight. But that didn't happen. We were going to have to do it with the neighborhood, with the left and the right, with people who had no influence but who did have a commitment to see a better neighborhood and city. And so I learned that when the government doesn't respond positively, then we just focus on our community."

The Reynolds District School Board showed that they were willing to kill a nationally ranked charter school in order to defend their entrenched systems. But that outrage mobilized hundreds of interconnected and educated neighbors. It felt as if success should break out. But there were also troubling stories coming back from our Speaks! and Knocks data. Of all of the ethnicities and races and countries and language groups of the soup of Rockwood, the stories from African Americans bothered me the most. I knew that the people of Gresham were rednecks, because I'd grown up with them. But were they racists too?

I needed some guides in the Black community who could answer these questions honestly and wisely.

CHAPTER 7

The Black Chapter

*M*y answering of emails was interrupted by a confident knock on the door of the new Rockwood CDC office, and Willie Chambers walked in. At the time, the Rockwood CDC was still using the shuttered barbershop as our office. We had closed down Foxy Girls, and next on the list was the check-cashing store and the hourly motel. I wasn't the only one working in this one-room office. There were always people coming and going, and we were so tight that we would often have two separate meetings going at two ends of the *same table.* Nevertheless, Willie and I found a place to have a conversation.

Social entrepreneurship ran in Willie's family as far as family memory allows. His people were in Tulsa, Oklahoma, in 1921 when "Black Wall Street," a thirty-five-square-block area that was home to America's wealthiest black community, was razed to the ground by mobs of whites, and Willie's newly impoverished family fled Oklahoma for south Los Angeles. The downstream devastation for Blacks has not stopped, much less healed.

"Willie, we are working to bring African Americans to the table, but it hasn't gone well. Creating a functioning community with full African American participation has unique challenges. What do I do?"

"I say that you start by listening to our stories. Learn who folks are, and what they want out of life here. There is history with people from my community. We should be saying, "Wow, this scab has been on here for 125 years, and it has never healed." Why? Because we never looked at it and talked about it."

Getting a small group of Black adults together in Rockwood took a while, but eventually fourteen gathered to talk. Scott McCracken, one of my teammates, invited people to dinner in his home. Scott and his wife, Vicki, had lived in Athens, Greece, for many years, and she rolled out one of her for-the-ages Greek dinners. I soon realized that most of the guests didn't know each other. When people are in a given geography because of serial forced displacement, they tend to not know their own neighbors. "I have a suggestion," Scott said. "We'll go around the room, and everyone gets eighteen minutes to tell their story. After that, everyone is welcome to ask clarifying questions, like 'When you said *that*, did you mean *this*?' but none of us is free to challenge the story. Obviously, Brad and I are the white guys in the room. We aren't going to say anything at all unless someone asks us to."

This practice of being quiet—all by itself—is a powerful environment changer. This is going to sound funny, but as a white CEO, I never knew that I wasn't always welcome to ask whatever questions I wanted to ask. I have been told since I was a boy that "active listening" was a sign of engagement and valuing and, well, respect. But only in Rockwood did I learn that when a power imbalance exists and the more powerful person just lets some questions remain unposed or unanswered, the less powerful person perceives that he has been respected. So, in that meeting in Scott's house, I just sat and listened in order to show respect.

"My family moved to Portland from Selma when my uncle got lynched," the first man began.

And this is how it *starts*? "My uncle got lynched" is how it *starts*? This man had my full and undivided attention, and I only grew more absorbed as his story spiraled downhill from there.

Not every storyteller had a harrowing tale. Two women in their sixties said that they had never personally experienced any form of discrimination or racism—a surprise to me.

"I too moved here about four years ago," said another man. "First I moved out to the Numbers, and it's rough. I was born in New York and lived my life from sixteen through thirty-something in Wisconsin. But moving here has been a culture shock for me because . . . listen— we know that it's there, we know that it exists . . . but even so, that has been a hard pill for me to swallow. I'm not disrespecting—I have my own stereotypes. But we have been bypassed and bypassed. We built this land too. It was from our work, and now we are begging for scraps."

This man referred to Rockwood as the Numbers because there are few identifying landmarks or commercial centers among the miles of East County homes and apartments. People who live here can't say that they live next to the county courthouse or the mall or just south of Mile Square Park. All anyone who lives here can say is that they live on 143rd, or 199th. Bland, grid-like, boring. You know, the Numbers.

"I'm not really from here," a young man said, "but I got to know Rockwood when my brother was shot on the street." Everyone listened hard as Vince told of his solid middle-class upbringing in

North Portland, the historic home of most Portland-area African American families. Although families like Vince's might be full of straight arrows, that doesn't prevent some family members from going off script, at least temporarily. No one knows how Vince's brother got involved in drugs, but there he was one day, deep in the Numbers, when the gun went off.

For four hours, we all listened as one person after another told their story. When everyone was through, I couldn't contain myself. "I know that I'm not supposed to say anything," I said, "but I have one question: When is the last time you told your story to a white guy?"

There was silence as everyone looked back at me, and then at each other. "I have never told my story to a white guy," Robert said. "None of you have ever asked."

Later, I told Dr. Peter Clark about this profound evening. One of Peter's professional projects is filming ultra-poor people in the developing world so that they may tell their story. "Brad," he said, "I'm a pretty good interviewer. I can walk into a slum, and after twenty minutes, I've established trust, and I've got local people, on camera, talking to a foreigner. I've always prided myself on being able to get people to talk.

"But I was in Delhi, India, interviewing a woman, and none of my usual tricks worked. I tried them all, and I never got more than a grunt. She wouldn't look me in the eye—she only looked down. I finally gave up and turned to our host, who is a social worker, very empathetic, working with an Indian microfinance company. 'Rajni, what's going on here?'

"'You must understand,' Rajni answered. 'This woman is a Dalit. She's the lowest class. She's from the bottom of the barrel in India, and she has probably never in her life had anyone, whether Indian or foreign, ask her about her personal feelings. And she is so disconnected from them, she probably has no words to express how she thinks and how she feels.'

"This blew me away. Think of a world full of people created in the image of God, shaped in the mind of God with dignity and self-worth. And yet somehow they have been reduced to the level of that Dalit woman who couldn't speak to me."

"And how does that relate to the neighbors I just spent the evening with?"

"My point, Brad, is: What is the functional difference in a culture between a Dalit who has no voice and an African American no one is listening to?"

The deep brokenness of my neighbors, both white and Black, did not happen in a vacuum, and it did not happen by accident. Portland's history of racism goes back to its founding. Oregon was admitted to the Union as a free state, but that did not mean that African Americans were welcome. It was illegal for them to move here, and this remained a feature of our state constitution until the 1920s. Each local municipality also had its own exclusion laws, sundown laws, poll taxes just for people of color, ways to deny voting rights, and exclusions from public school. The first half of the twentieth century brought redlining and segregation during a period when Oregon had the largest membership in the KKK per capita of any state in the US. Our national history books showcase the virulent racism and terrorism of the South, but in many ways the silent innocence of Portland is more dishonest.

What is the difference between a Dalit who has no voice and an African-American no one is listening to?"

The World War II years finally revealed the hearts of white leaders. The story of the federal government's illegal treatment of Japanese Americans is well known. But what is less well known is that when the internment camps were emptied in 1945 and the Japanese Americans returned to their homes and farms in Gresham, they were not welcomed back. Gresham's then mayor co-founded "Oregon Anti-Japanese, Inc.," which worked to change state law so that the city could seize these assets. A thousand people turned up at a rally at Gresham High School in 1945 to deny returning Japanese Americans their property rights, and the speeches were so outrageous that even the *New York Times* covered the story with a reference to the return of the KKK in my community.

During those same war years, Portland's African American population grew quickly, and thousands lived in a temporary North Portland neighborhood called Vanport. They lived there because redlining policies prevented them from living anywhere else. When Vanport flooded, displacing thousands from their homes, the Albina District became the refugee area of town.

I was born in 1962, when my family lived in a house right between the demolished Vanport and the new Albina. My life began as it is still today—deeply entwined with race. I have people on my family tree who were slave owners. Others were abolitionists. My ancestors fought on both sides of the Civil War. Some were members of the KKK, into the 1970s, and others were deeply involved in racial justice work during the same years. But I didn't know about Portland's racism, because when I was five, my folks moved out to Rockwood from the inner city as part of a larger "white flight" trend. So when big sections of Albina were razed for a hospital expansion (the same hospital I was born in) my family didn't directly feel the effects. Nineteen blocks of Black homes and businesses were wiped out without community involvement, for an expansion that never happened. Many of those blocks are weed fields to this day. Where did displaced African American people go? At first in drips and then in a rush, they moved out to the Numbers.

The Numbers did not welcome the new neighbors. In those days Rockwood wasn't a part of Gresham, nor was it a part of Portland. It was in unincorporated Multnomah County, which meant that there was little land use planning, or building code enforcement, or even paved streets. Rents were the lowest in the metro area, which meant that displaced families could afford the Numbers. What a disaster it was when desperately needy families moved into a white-flight neighborhood with no amenities, no social services, and no desire to make life welcoming. People were set back a whole generation or more. And no one knew or cared.

One day I was working in the little barbershop office when in walked a politician. This veteran of public office was running for county commissioner and wanted the support of the Rockwood CDC. Decades before, he had been on the Portland City Council when the decision to destroy the center of Black life at Albina was made. "That decision has had major ramifications for thousands of vulnerable people," I told him. "Looking back at it, what do you think of the, uh, the unintended consequences of your decision?"

"Unintended?" he snorted. "There were no unintended consequences. We knew exactly what we were doing. Portland needed to win the war on poverty. The government had millions of dollars for us if we could drive incomes up. Well, the easiest way to do that is to drive poor people out. As long as they went across the city line into unincorporated county, then we won the war on poverty!"

I couldn't believe my ears.

I knew the assistant secretary of the US Department of Housing and Urban Development during that period, a man whose region of responsibility included Portland. I told him what the politician in Rockwood had told me. "Dick," I asked him, "could it possibly be true that this human disaster was intentional?"

"Absolutely, Brad. This was how the War on Poverty was waged. Our attention in Washington was on-again, off-again. We had to get rid of a *lot* of money fast. We just ended up having to trust people like Neil Goldschmidt, your mayor, to do the best he could."

"In other words, Dick, the systems aren't broken, even though the intended recipients of the benefits of those systems might believe they are. They're working just as they were designed to."

"Yup."

Early on in our relationship, I never knew whether my new friends like Willie wanted to hear this stuff. Even though this is how they imagine white leaders talk to each other when Black people aren't in the room, they don't really believe that these conversations are so blatant and so callous. When I tell them that these conversations are indeed that cold—and even colder—they get a sad little smirk that says, *I knew it*.

> **The systems aren't broken. They're working just as they were designed to.**

Willie wanted to hear the truth, and I laid it out for him plain. "What effect has this had on the African American community's ability to address its own problems?" I asked.

"There are members of the Black community who have been dissected or severed from North Portland to where they are now out here in Rockwood," he said.

"Is this why every once in a while we get a call from one of the historically African American organizations in Portland, wondering if *I* can introduce them to some Black people? I mean, that's messed up."

"Right. There are *members*, but there is no *body* that speaks for the whole. I hate to look back to the old Albina neighborhood for an example, but at least they had some structure there. We have to build trust again, despite the past, or else there is no going forward. And that trust can't be in the Rockwood CDC or in some project. It has to be built amongst ourselves, on the basis of shared purpose. Realistically, we have a long way to go yet."

In a lot of ways, the history of Rockwood since the 1970s got even sadder. As the population grew, due to displacement from Portland, so did violence and poverty. Violence and poverty do not have to go hand in hand, but in this case they did, because the attitude of the leaders of the area was disdain and even outright hatred.

THE POLICE

In 2013, I met with the city of Gresham's police chief to talk about Rockwood. We spent a few minutes exchanging notes on the high level of violence, and then I asked him what my organization could do to help reinforce his efforts. The chief leaned back in his chair and said, "Well, if it was up to me, I would build a wall around Rockwood and let them all just fucking shoot each other!"

I blinked in disbelief. I had no ready response—after all, my purpose then was not to confront but to build bridges. I wasn't even sure if the obvious interpretation of his words was the correct one— until a couple of weeks later when he was speaking at a public event I attended. During a question-and-answer session, the chief was asked if he had hired more officers who brought diversity to his staff. "Yes, I did. I now have an Asian, a Latino, and a Black."

That's a pretty good start, I thought.

"I call 'em my little bag of M&M's," he said with a self-satisfied smile. Talk about snatching defeat from the jaws of victory. Anywhere else, a public comment like that would have gotten the chief fired. But in Gresham, this was par for the course.

People in Gresham feel (rightly) that Portland forced its problem on them. In 1987, Rockwood was annexed into Gresham by state court order against the wishes of people in both Gresham and Rockwood. The result is that the Gresham city government wants to get rid of a third of its citizens. People in Rockwood are not succeeding because the city of which they are a part does not *want* them to succeed. Their housing policy shows that. The city wants them gone.

All of us at the Rockwood CDC went through a period of grieving the truth of our community and talking carefully about what steps we could take. After all, *reconciliation* is one of our four core values. As we processed together, a picture emerged along two fronts. The first was the need for a lot of Level One and Two Rockwood Speaks! sessions. The other was Level Three: We would assist Black leaders in setting up their own boards and structure, and even encourage them to develop new nonprofits. Our hope was that in this way our Black neighbors could speak for themselves and control their own narrative.

I was glad that by this time Rockwood Speaks! was well refined, and that we could use it to do facilitated listening. The issue that African Americans were most concerned about was policing—not surprising because, at a national level, injustice at the hands of police was evident.[4] In 2016, we partnered with a local Black pastor and consultant to the city to create a Speaks! Level Two set of conversations around the police and Rockwood's African Americans. This connected members of the Gresham police department to the neighbors, primarily from communities of color, whom they protect and serve.

Getting the police department to the table shouldn't have been a tough sell. According to the report that the City Council commissioned, the police had already been formally instructed to "generate an open dialogue about race and culture, employ a workforce made up of people from diverse backgrounds, deliver services in equitable systems, and engage with the community in an inclusive, equitable, and authentic way." The format was simple. The series ran one night per month and featured just two or three open-ended questions that were designed to generate truth telling and empathy on both sides.

At the start of one of the earliest sessions, at which then-Deputy Chief Sells was in attendance, one of the attending officers interrupted to say, "Who the fuck are you?" and to ask who he was "to tell me what to do." In a later session, a police captain gave a different officer a homework assignment: to research the grand jury decision that followed the killing of Michael Brown in Ferguson, Missouri, and report back with an opinion so that he could discuss "rationally" whether that officer was justified in using deadly force.

Despite those problems, the very frustrated Black pastor and facilitator pressed on with us. I was thrilled to see many off-duty officers attend without being paid, and thrilled also that many of my neighbors attended to listen and interact. Many officers told of their long personal connection to Rockwood, and many neighbors told of their respect for the police. I learned something new every single night. For example, one night people were talking about how to de-escalate routine traffic stops. One young black man named David said that he really didn't understand the fuss. "After all," he said, "when I'm stopped, I just follow the protocol."

"What do you mean—protocol?" someone asked from across the room.

"You know. You turn off the ignition and lay the keys on the dash. You turn on the dome light and turn off the music. You roll down all the windows. Then you put your driver's license and registration on the dash, and lay your hands palm up on the dash so that the officer can see that you're not holding anything. You know. That's normal. The protocol."

Several African American parents were nodding, and the police were smiling. But for me, it took a second for the protocol to sink in.

"David," I said, "I raised four sons in this neighborhood too, and one of them is your age. I never taught him a protocol. It never occurred to me. I mean, there is a zero percent chance that one of my sons, as white young men, will be pulled over in a routine traffic stop that escalates into him being shot in the back. In my house, there is no protocol because there's no need for one."

Now it was David's turn to process. He looked down for a moment, and when he looked up, there were tears in his eyes. "I . . . uh, I thought precautions like this were normal. I just realized that even though, like you, I am educated and solid middle class, I am not a part of this neighborhood in the same way that *you* are part of this neighborhood." David looked at me somberly. "I am really *not* like your son. Am I?"

The Speaks! series was exciting and groundbreaking when we had breakthroughs like that, but most of the time it remained stubbornly mundane. Our facilitator tried everything he could think of to get people to *really* tell the truth, but it just wasn't happening. After a few months of this, many of us were questioning the usefulness of continuing.

One evening I thought of a tack that might help rip the scab off the wound. I had learned that in just about every police department in the country, a close analysis of the statistics will reveal bias. Even if few cops are racists, the little acts of unconscious bias at every level of the system accumulate into the shocking disproportionality at the level of felonies and even executions.[5] I phoned ahead and asked the officer at headquarters if he would come to the next Speaks! session and show us where the Gresham police were in their attempts to wring bias out of the system.

When the evening came, the officer showed up empty-handed. "Officer, we need to see your numbers," I said.

"Well, we don't keep records about race when it comes to our police department actions."

"You don't?" I said. "The city council requires you to, and it's also state law. You have to. Why don't you?"

"Well, years ago, we noticed that the statistics we were capturing showed that we don't have a problem. So we stopped."

They don't have a problem because they don't keep data. This is a city of 110,000 people.

After he said this, two African Americans in the group stood and walked out.

As facilitators, we have an obligation to stop hosting Speaks! sessions if it's clear that they're only going to damage the community further. We held a couple more sessions on this topic, but after that exchange about bias, I knew that we would be staring at a blue wall for a long time to come. A few months later, a young Black man was murdered in a racially charged hate crime just a hundred feet from where these conversations were happening. We did not reconvene after that.

The story of how Portland and Gresham have harmed people because of the color of their skin has become well-known in recent years. But somehow, it still hasn't sunk in with my former classmates and church members that all of us in the white community bear responsibility for this.

The Centennial School District is one of three that serve Rockwood. It was originally named the Lynch District because, in pioneer days, a family with that name donated an acre of their forty-acre land claim so that a school could be built. I was a first-grader at Lynch Plaza Elementary, and the other five schools in the district each bore Lynch as their first name. There were between zero and two African American kids in the whole district during those years, but it is 73 percent minority now. My teachers were blissfully ignorant of the history of race in our area, and they liked it that way.

I remember as a second-grader being enamored with cowboys and Indians. All of the stories and TV shows I loved seemed to be set in the Southwest. Did we have cool stories about Oregon too? "No," my teacher said, "there weren't any Indians here. Oh, maybe a few, but they were mostly gone because of smallpox by the time the Oregon Trail came through."

That wasn't true, of course. Lynch Plaza sits on land that we stole from Native Americans while they were suffering from the ravages of the disease. My own great-grandfather traveled up and down the nearby Columbia River in 1905, teaching literacy to native kids. The level of ignorance about white culture's complicity in unnecessary human suffering never fails to raise my anger.

Today, the Black kids in this school district are often unwelcome and are subject to bullying by students and teachers alike. The school board, knowing that they had to take action, decided, among other things, to remove the word "Lynch" from the school names. I knew at least one family in the district whose great uncle had been lynched, so the name change seemed like a small but visible move in the right direction. As soon as the name change was announced, all hell broke loose on Facebook and other media platforms:

"Ridiculous."

"We lose too much when we don't keep our history alive."

"Oh no! Very sad."

"Shortsighted and disrespectful."

"This is the dumbest thing ever."

"The name is perfectly fine."

"Historical revisionism that liberals practice!"

"It sounds to me like some stupid jerk got offended."

"Get thick-skinned!"

"I hope they get rid of the rope in the gym before someone gets lynched."

"We were here long before you were."

In the end, the school board did the right thing and changed the name of the schools.

If Level One and Level Two conversations were disheartening and even harmful, I had more hope for the Level Three conversations. One of the assets that we could build on was the presence of elders in the African American community who had lived through the displacement and wanted to advise the younger and more action-oriented Black leaders.

Willie is one of those elders. "There is a unity amongst African Americans that has not been solidified. We are siloed, and folks in government want to keep us that way. We have not coalesced to say, 'Here is what we are going to do together in Portland and Gresham.' The jury is still out, but my hope is that future generations will understand that they need the wisdom of the elders. I'm really skeptical of the new energies coming in and saying, 'We're the voice of the community.' That's my major concern."

My observation is that Rockwood's leaders are still living in the long-standing tension between two camps. One identifies with the principles of Rev. Dr. Martin Luther King Jr., who called the flourishing community the "beloved community." The other identifies with radical and direct action. One camp seems resolute, patient, and intentional about pushing the system toward an inevitable just conclusion, while the other camp demands change now. This was the fault line in Civil War times, and during Reconstruction, and Jim Crow, and the Civil Rights era of the 1960s, and in Gresham today. This isn't my fight to make, but whenever I am asked to participate, I will do everything that I can do to move the conversation to the beloved community.

I asked Willie who fills the social capital vacuum. Is it the social service agencies, the church, clubs, the government? I tell him that I see the culturally specific social service agencies trying to create community, but they rarely succeed.

Willie jumped right in. "They aren't designed to lead. They're designed to say, 'We'll take care of you. We'll pay for your health care, we'll pay for groceries.' Well, where does my personal responsibility fit in? 'Don't worry, we'll take care of it,' the agencies say. But it's not the government's place, or the agencies that they pay, to take care of everyone. We have to create for ourselves the structure that is going to foster real relationships, land ownership, and healthy families."

Over the years, Willie and many others like Vince have taken runs at creating a new web of social capital. Some went under within a couple of months, some are there in name only, some are really only a couple of people, and others are becoming broad and stable. At the end of the day, none of these are about me—and all of them, if they succeed, need to succeed on their own. Which is good, because I want to give up. Maybe that's just my privilege, because if I give up, nothing changes for me—I just live as always in my racist culture as a white guy. But if *they* give up, if they're unable to establish reliable social capital for and by the African American community, they give up on the prospect of flourishing for them and their descendants.

Willie has done the most to help me stay engaged. "Brad, somewhere love has to be the foundation that we function from, because that's how they'll know there is something different about these people. They are taking care of each person who has need. Language has nothing to do with it. Race has nothing to do with it. Income has nothing to do with it. Each person has worth because they are made in the image of God. Rockwood to me is ground zero for the beloved community."

I pray that he is right.

CHAPTER 8

Place Matters

I was deep in a conversation with an Eritrean refugee who was starting a cleaning business when my phone rang. On the other end was Josh, the city of Gresham's urban renewal director. "Are you sitting down?" he asked. "The Black Cat Cantina is shutting down next week, and when they reopen, they're going to be a strip club!"

My heart sank. We had just closed down the Foxy Girls Club, which had left my vulnerable community with no explicit sex trafficking businesses. And now, right next door to where the Foxy Girls had been, the evil industry would regain a foothold in our neighborhood. Doing some homework, I learned that the new strip club wouldn't be just any strip club. It would be an extension of a chain well known for human sex trafficking. This location, in fact, was to be their new flagship store.

The Black Cat was next door to my Sunrise Development project and right across the street from the city's new $40 million urban renewal project. If a major strip club got embedded, both the city of Gresham and the Rockwood CDC knew that we could kiss our projects goodbye.

I hadn't thought it important to build a physical community center in Rockwood. So far, all of our work was taking place in our office, in parks, and in the meeting rooms at apartment complexes. I knew of large nonprofits in North Portland that had built palaces, but when the population that they served moved, their multimillion-dollar asset could not move with them. Several of these institutions served African Americans, but those clients had moved out to the Numbers long ago. So it was not uncommon for buses to troll my neighborhood and pick up kids to bring them to after-school programs an hour away. I didn't want the Rockwood CDC to be in a similar position years later when poverty moved and my building could not move with it. But I also knew from Rockwood Speaks! that my neighbors needed a community center. Portland has shown that it is willing to fund the creation of great centers, but Gresham is not. I was intrigued. Here was a perfectly good, 12,500-square-foot building about to be repurposed in the most negative of ways. Could it be repurposed in a positive direction instead? "What is the City going to do?" I asked Josh.

"Nothing. We can't shut down the strip club because stripping is protected free speech in Oregon. As long as they keep serving food, their existing restaurant license is all they need. Maybe *you* can talk to them."

I set up a meeting to talk to the owner of the property the next day, with no idea of what I would say. It was clear that he wasn't really interested in the stripping business. Rather, this was a last-ditch effort to avoid a financial disaster that would cause him to lose the building to foreclosure.

"I'm not sure that stripping alone is going to help me save this place," he said, brazenly honest. "But once the drug business gets going in the parking lot, that will drive a lot of profits." As I listened, the term *bottom feeder* came to mind. But in reality, Oregon's poorest community had a number of other land and building owners who were just like this guy: slumlords, unlicensed businesses, black-market dealers, payday loan companies, plasma centers, video poker pods, and strip clubs that are far more evident in Rockwood than they are anywhere else.

"Would you consider, instead, just selling this place?" I asked.

"I would entertain an offer for the building. I want $1.35 million."

"Good! I'd like to buy it. The only problem is, I don't really *have* $1.35 million. In fact…I don't really have one-point-three-five dollars. But if you'll lease this building to me for one year, with an option to purchase it for that amount, I'll sign that deal."

To my complete surprise, the owner agreed and drew up the contract.

I had been warned that he would try stunts both legal and illegal to get my money without actually giving up the building—like "forgetting" to record the sale documents, forging notes, and other slimy tactics. And yes, he tried them all. It was the first time I saw with my own eyes that a low-income, poorly educated population of neighbors cannot, by themselves, complete the transactions neces-sary to rid their business districts of exploitative businesspeople. They must be assisted by justice-oriented professionals who will defend them.

So the huge space, formerly a Mexican restaurant, came into my control. The lease was $7,000 a month, beyond the capacity of my donor base. I would have to sublease it. But to whom, I had no idea.

Leasing the building was very risky, but getting a stuck commu-nity unstuck sometimes requires someone to shoulder an inordi-nately large load. There were some things going in our favor, and others going against us. The negatives were that I would have to find short-term tenants willing to move out in less than a year and also that we could not afford to remodel the building for our needs. The positives were that it would be a big step forward for the community and that it was consistent with our vision/mission as an organization. Also, the CDC had no money invested in it, so if I failed to make the lease payment after five months, then I would still have forestalled the strip club by five months. And that, undoubtedly, is what the building owner thought would happen. It was also possible that, at the end of the day, the building would generate a positive cash flow that could enable the CDC to at last be stable.

As soon as I signed the lease, I began fundraising for the needed $1.35 million. We launched a capital campaign, but it went nowhere. I had hoped that the big-money people who had stiff-armed me so far would have my back when it mattered, and this mattered. But even though I had a hot-button issue to sell (eliminating stripping and narcotics), *no one* would donate toward the acquisition. Trying to punch up the appeal, I named it the Sunrise Center and created a nifty logo. I wrote vision statements and recruited sub-tenants to occupy the space. A church moved into the former bar, a large Latino social service agency rooted in North Portland established their first colony in the Numbers, and people booked parties and meetings. Although there were great things happening every day at the Sunrise Center, many of them for the first time in Rockwood, wealthy people and philanthropies were just not responding. Soon it was the eleventh month, and the end of my purchase option was looming. On June 30, we would have to kick everybody out and close the doors. By June 15, I had raised a grand total of $5,000. With two weeks to go, I was still $1,345,000 short.

And then the phone rang. It was Josh, Gresham's urban renewal director. "Are you sitting down?"

"Again? Yes. Every time you call, I just sit. What's up?"

"Well, as you know, my fiscal budget ends on June 30. I have operating accounts, and I have capital accounts. The funds in the capital accounts must be zeroed out by June 30, and the only way to do that is on land acquisition or major improvements to buildings."

"Okay, I'm familiar with how your accounting works. I'm still not sure why I had to sit down to hear this."

"A couple of years ago, the urban renewal division sold some excess land on contract. The buyers just decided to pay off the contract early. Two million dollars just dropped into my capital account. And remember, that money can only be used on land acquisition or major building improvements. With only two weeks to go in the fiscal year, it's too late to get a deal done. So my thought is that you might have an idea how, in under two weeks, I can get rid of some of that money in a way that benefits the taxpayers."

"As a matter of fact, I do. My option to purchase the Sunrise Center is assignable to another party, so I could assign it to you. Then you could buy it. I figure that, the way property prices are going up in Portland, that building is worth at least $1.7 million on the open market, so you lock in a gain on day one."

Within a week, and with just one week to go on my option to buy, the Sunrise Center was under contract. We had saved the neighborhood from disaster after all!

Now it was my turn to pose a question to Josh: "Congratulations on your new real estate transaction. What are you going to do with it?"

"Do you have any ideas?"

"As a matter of fact, I do," I said. "Lease it to us and we'll continue to use it for community benefit until a long-term plan for the site is in place."

So we signed a five-year lease for $2,000 a month (the first year was free!) and continued operations as if no interruption had ever loomed. I had originally been skeptical about being able to raise all of that money for an asset that I didn't even want. As it turned out, I didn't have to raise a penny.

My white-knuckle ride was over—for a while, at least. What had I learned? That it takes someone willing to be the point of the spear. Once that person has assumed the risk, others come along. I had a lawyer who protected me, an urban renewal director who enabled me, and scores of neighbors who would buy space from me if I secured it. My ultimate goal was not to make money. It was to give life to a dark place. To reproduce life in others. To draw ever-expanding networks of people into the Sunrise Center, people drawn to it because it was interesting. It showed my neighbors that transformation requires risk. It sent up a signal flare that could be seen all over Portland that this liminal place, this place that was literally outside the city walls, this place that no one inside the city walls cared about, might no longer be a place of disgrace. In fact, this place might be more alive than anywhere else in Portland.

When the Mexicans from the State of Michoacán who lived in Rockwood wanted to mount a huge fiesta, they used our Sunrise Center. People from this fractured community of Mexicans drove all the way from Eastern Washington and Northern California to celebrate with dance, food, and family. They spilled out into the parking lot with an elaborate dance between a man in a twelve-foot-tall bull costume and another man in a ten-foot-tall toreador costume. The mariachi band had seventeen costumed members. I was told that this was the most authentic Michoacánan celebration in America.

The church that met in the Sunrise Center for the first year stayed. And then a second one rented space on Sunday nights. Then a third squeezed in on Sunday afternoons. *Hundreds* of people flowed through the Center every single week. The reach of their relief projects was staggering—clothes closets, food pantries, counseling services, spiritual renewal, family reconciliation, engagement in justice issues, and coordination with the social service agencies sprang up naturally from these energetic and newly unleashed neighbors.

The local Head Start preschool needed someone to cook hot breakfasts and lunches, and we stepped up because we had a massive commercial kitchen—given that this space had formerly been a restaurant. We hired Cecille, a Native-American mom who lives in Rockwood with her nine kids. She and her kids were sleeping in a homeless shelter when we hired her. Cecille managed the contract and her team like a pro—which wasn't easy, because the rest of her kitchen team was homeless or close to it. They were single moms just like Cecille who wanted out of poverty. Cecille and her team plated 51,000 meals in nine months for three-, four-, and five-year-olds who likely received on those plates the only balanced and healthy meals they would eat that day.

We finally had a place where everyone could learn, earn, and belong. We helped our neighbors belong by reducing isolation. We helped earners by reducing the gap from ambition to achievement. We engaged volunteers from outside Rockwood in meaningful ways. Seemingly out of nowhere, retired executives offered to coach our young entrepreneurs. A men's group from a local church renovated the upstairs with walled offices so that people could get businesses started. A local bank that was downsizing gave us eight fully equipped cubicles to provide local entrepreneurs with incubator space. An employee team from the National Forest Service renovated our warehouse.

We finally had a place where everyone could learn, earn, and belong.

I was astonished to see just how much *place matters*. Once the community had an open, welcoming, and affordable place, they filled the vacuum with their own expression of cultural life. Place matters. Because there was a new place, groups had an anchor, a place to call home, a place to congregate. When an Oregon State University economics professor wanted to launch a new financial product for low-income people, he chose the Center because of its location in Rockwood. The National Institutes of Health rented our parking lot for a public health outreach because we *had* a parking lot. The life of the Sunrise Center exactly matched the contours of the one hundred groups that called Rockwood home. I expect that when we establish our next Sunrise Center in another community, it will look and feel differently than the first one does because we will be true to the unique characteristics of *that* community.

Because place matters, and because we are promoting holistic human flourishing, natural links formed between unrelated groups and programs when people ran into each other at the Sunrise Center. Tafaoata came from American Samoa with her husband and four children. Her dream was to start her own business, selling hand-printed fabric and garments. She enrolled in our Rockwood English Language Institute, and after eight weeks, she was feeling more confident in her reading and writing and her ability to understand spoken English. She told me that she's now better able to understand the information that comes home from school with her kids, and she feels more comfortable communicating with their teachers and helping with homework. One of our Rockwood Works business counselors was able to give her some simple, concrete steps for moving forward with her business plan. At one of our traditional culture festivals, she confidently sold her Samoan prints and turned a profit. If she continues to have opportunities to build her confidence (including English class), we think she can accomplish her goals.

The only criticism I receive from the community is that there isn't enough Sunrise Center to go around. Before it opened, people had limited choices for public meeting space. Libraries are, for many communities, the most public space they have. Some communities also possess semipublic spaces like childcare centers, common areas in apartments, schools, parks, senior centers, and churches. If I had my way, a modern-day Andrew Carnegie would start building community centers instead of libraries in liminal neighborhoods all across America.

At the Sunrise Center, I don't provide much direct programming. I emphasize that the Sunrise Center is a shell that can be filled by just about anyone for any positive purpose. Prices are lower for Rockwood residents and much more expensive for Portland residents. All of the meeting rooms are booked every night. An elder day care for Slavic refugees occupies most of the weekdays. Parties are booked months in advance. I have learned that every ethnic group wants exclusivity because in an unequal society, these marginalized groups want access to a private space to be themselves before engaging other groups. Closed doors facilitate bonding. A couple of groups have demanded that the city give *them* the Sunrise Center instead of the white guy that they "gave" it to. For now, there is only one Sunrise Center and it will have to be shared by everyone.

Food preparation has emerged as a major activity. The Sunrise Center kitchen is an incubator that houses fifteen or so young businesses at a time. Even though food (as I have learned) is a lousy way for most people to build wealth, it can be an excellent on-ramp for people to have their first entrepreneurial experience. Our kitchen has food makers from Fiji, Guatemala, Romania, Brazil, Somalia, Japan, and the Mexican states of Ixtapa, Michoacán, and Chiapas. There are vegans and pulled-pork producers, a chocolatier and a soup maker, caterers, food truck proprietors, and bakers. Some have succeeded and moved on to bigger success, and others have folded.

On any given day, there are a dozen or more different cultural groups at work at the Center. And I promise you that several of them never planned on being in the same room as others. Sometimes my wife, Lynn, or Willie Chambers, in his role as the kitchen manager, sound like skilled conflict negotiators. How would you handle it when at one end of the kitchen there is a team of Japanese sushi makers huddled over their intricate and completely sanitary artwork, while at the other end a Somali stew maker throws a goat carcass on the floor for processing? "Khadro!" Lynn shouted. "You cannot throw a dead goat on the floor and start chopping it up. That isn't up to code for a commissary kitchen in the US. I'll bet that you can't even do that in Somalia!" While Khadro shouted his response, a Ukrainian sandwich maker walked by and sniffed. Since I don't personally have to manage the swirl that is the Sunrise Center kitchen, I have the luxury of just thinking that days like this are a lot of fun.

The success of the Sunrise Center propelled the Rockwood CDC into a new realm. In one year, our organizational chart grew to twenty-two people, representing ten full-time-equivalent positions. The budget hit $700,000. There was media attention and statewide acclaim. I had a lot of churn with staff members and partners, a process that feels like kissing lots of frogs to find a prince. I brought lots of moneyed donors through the Center to show them what is possible, but these meetings usually just revealed that the stark disconnect between the top 5 percent and the bottom 50 percent was too much of a bridge to build. Many of those wealthy potential donors would look at me as if I were a crazy visionary. I told them that what they were seeing at the Sunrise Center was not optimism, nor was it pessimism. It was a hard-nosed choice to create a new future.

One evening I told Lynn about my growing conviction that place mattered, and that having *a* place mattered too. But I was a product of the ether, of social media, of using digital tools to do business globally. The gears in my head were a little bit jammed up with the local—indeed hyperlocal—nature of the explosion of creativity and flourishing in Rockwood.

"That juxtaposition is something we understand well in the realm of community health," she said. "Even though medicine has advanced in a major way, do you know what has saved the most lives? Public health. Fixing the zip code has much more down-stream benefit for more people than any specific clinical treatment of a problem ever will."

"Downstream?"

"Remember in the Philippines, that village where the elementary school was on the other side of a river from the houses? The kids were using a cable to wade across it every day, and someone was always slipping. The farmers who worked downstream would try to fish them out and save them. We raised money and built a bridge so that the kids could just cross the bridge to walk to school. We fixed the upstream problem so that the downstream problem no longer appeared. To pay attention to upstream issues, you have to look at specific social and economic factors that eventually lead to poor health outcomes. Problems with upstream issues explain why, in Rockwood, far too many people die young."

I learned from Lynn that the upstream issues are broadly grouped into twelve categories:

- income and social status
- employment and working conditions
- education and literacy
- childhood experiences
- physical environments
- social supports and coping skills
- healthy behaviors
- access to health services
- biology and genetic endowment
- gender
- culture
- race and racism

Some of the factors on that list I could do something about; others remain beyond my reach.

Lynn's thoughts about the social determinants of health challenged me to think deeply, because as a middle- to upper-middle-class white man, I think a lot more about an individual's personal, internal ownership of their health. I was raised to think that if people's heads and hearts are right, then good behavior and prosperity will follow. While there is some truth to that, the public health world thinks more about the built environment. I could readily see from the Sunrise Center just how much impact a little building has on the shalom of the neighborhood.

I believe that this distinction is at the heart of our national health care discussion in America today. When it comes to our understanding of poverty, of suffering, of inequalities and inequities, some of us are about systems, and others of us are about individuals:

How We Think about Our Low-Income Neighbors		
	If You're Systems-Oriented, You Think ...	If You're Individual-Oriented, You Think ...
People flourish because ...	Their environment is right.	Their head and heart are right.
People don't flourish because ...	Low-income people face barriers to accessing resources that more privileged people do not face.	They have not taken personal ownership.

The other side ...	Requires obedience to their cultural norms before they help the poor. This is evil.	Takes our money through taxes so that they can make the poor dependent on them. This is evil.
We won't stop until ...	Everyone enjoys the same level of flour- ishing. This is justice.	Everyone experi- ences redemption. This is love.
The flaws that people from the other side cannot see are ...	Just because someone's head and heart are right doesn't mean that they rise into pros- perity. And "right" is a cultural construct created by people who want to stay in power.	Massive govern- ment investment in poverty hasn't worked. Forcing me to fund their agenda is their way to stay in power.

I knew, going into the creation of the holistic development work in Rockwood, that if I am not doing it *all*, then I am not doing it *at all*. This means that *both* the head/heart and the environment must be working together to create a community that promotes human flourishing. Both the "bottom up" work and the "top down" work are needed. The first few years of my work here were all about the "bottom up" and not much about the "top down." My "top down" effort, the Sunrise Development project, had hit roadblock after roadblock put there by people who didn't want change. My partner- ship was straining under the load, and my partners seemed ready to abandon the project. I could sense a backlash brewing at the city too. How could I be proud of my civic engagement work if all

I did was lead these vulnerable neighbors into a brick wall? I grew increasingly convinced that unless I could unleash a major "top down" strategy, the hard reality was that the flourishing community would remain just a dream. But how in the world could I do that?

And then I thought of my friend David Doig, CEO of the Chicago Neighborhood Initiative. He's in the middle of one of America's largest and most holistic transformations of a town: Pullman on Chicago's far South Side.

"David, can I come see you?"

"Sure! I love to show off what we've done. Come on out."

I met up with David in his modest office in the heart of the neighborhood on a hot summer day in sweltering Chicagoland. "Brad, since we started in 2010, we've put almost $400 million to work in this one community, and we aren't done."

"I've put $1.35 million worth of capital to use," I said. "Yours is a staggeringly large amount of capital. What have you done with it?"

"Oh, man, let's drive around and see."

I wanted to see what could be done to create *place*, and I wasn't disappointed. We jumped into David's car and drove around the 180 acres of Pullman, a historically significant, predominantly African American community. David and his team of just six people arranged the financing and solicited community support for a complete transformation of Pullman. How? By harnessing $150 million of New Markets Tax Credits (a US Department of the Treasury program that incentivizes community development and economic growth in distressed communities by offering tax credits to private investors) with $250 million of incentives from Chicago, commercial debt, and private-equity investments. While all of that is sophisticated and hard, it isn't impossible. There are professionals in each of America's cities who are capable of orchestrating capital at this scale if they just had the vision to do so.

David and his team used this money to build more than a million square feet of commercial and retail space. They built a massive new community and recreation center. There are scores of new houses, condos, and apartments. They even created a new national monument that honors the history of Pullman.

David is a quiet and unassuming guy, so I had to drag out of him what sort of impact his work was having.

"Huge," he finally admitted. "We've created 4,665 jobs and counting. We have lent money to 117 businesses to enable their growth. Residential property values are up 136 percent. These are numbers that no one—probably including me—thought possible."

Our national ongoing discussion about the effects of gentrification certainly came to mind when I was talking to David. The loudest voices belong to social justice warriors and the media, who bemoan the harm to low-income people of color when a neighborhood suddenly fills up with rich white people. It is funny that "the g word" has been a persistent theme over the last five years, because most of America's underinvested neighborhoods don't have that problem at all. I asked David about Pullman's experience with gentrification.

"There are certainly some neighborhoods in Chicago that are experiencing some price and rent appreciation," he said. "But that's probably limited to ten to twelve neighborhoods in a city of seventy-seven neighborhoods. Call that 10 percent to 15 percent of Chicago's neighborhoods. The larger narrative that we are experiencing here in Chicago is the issue of depopulation and out-migration. Certainly in the communities I've worked in in the past thirty years, the issue of gentrification has been secondary to a larger narrative. The issue, the larger story, in most of urban America, is depopulation. This is also true in rural America.

"There are two kinds of displacement.[6] You've got displacement from *lack* of development, which has been the story of the south and west side of Chicago. And then you've got displacement *because* of development. In neighborhoods with a housing stock of two-flats or three-flats, you are seeing people converting them into single-family homes. That's pushing displacement a little, but not much."

"So, in Pullman, you haven't had an out-migration? Why?" I asked.

"Our housing stock doesn't really lend itself to that kind of gentrification. These are small row houses that always provided working-class, affordable housing. You just can't turn a Pullman row house into a million-dollar rehab."

Indeed, the data shows that there are only five US cities—Portland, Seattle, Atlanta, Washington, DC, and maybe Denver—in which college-educated white people are displacing low-income people in suburban neighborhoods, so I hear a lot about it where I live. As a community developer, I know that our success in transforming a neighborhood sometimes causes the very people that we were trying to help to instead move out. Families are devastated as a result. This narrative is so strong that it is driving local officials to draft new (and sometimes so-old-it's-new) housing policies. It sounds reasonable that rent controls, inclusionary zoning, price supports, and other interventions could stem the tide of displaced families.

Just one problem. When you do the math, you find out that gentrification isn't inherently bad.[7] Really. Almost all revitalization in America is equitable. And although it's counternarrative, studies show that very few families are hurt when a neighborhood gentrifies, and the vast majority benefit. It's easy to understand that house and business owners benefit greatly from rising property prices. But what about the renters, who don't? Studies show that at the lowest tier of income, renters move around a lot. Even in a non-gentrifying neighborhood, over a ten-year period, 60 to 70 percent of renters move on, move out, move up, or move down. For most, life is transition—and for the poorest, life is triage. Whether the rents in a particular neighborhood are rising or dropping makes little difference to their long-term flourishing.

But this is not true of all renters. Some higher-income renters are able to rise with their neighborhoods. They benefit from higher wages and more business formation. They form new social capital with people who are better off. And their kids benefit from public schools that are getting better.

This last point is not trivial. The public schools in Rockwood are among the worst in the nation. Alder Elementary down the street ranks #1,193 out of Oregon's 1,194 schools. Only 6 percent of third-graders at Alder can do third-grade math. But change is coming to Alder Elementary, because newly displaced families from Portland's gentrification wave are moving in.

I said to one of the school district's senior administrative officers, "You guys cannot possibly be okay with Alder. What is your plan to fix it?"

"Oh, I don't see a lot of hand-wringing at the head office. Gentrification will fix the school for us. We just need to run out the clock."

Callous? Terrible? Perhaps—but in another sense, it's very realistic. Those kids whose families can hang in there against rising rent prices will themselves run out the clock and end up attending a much better school. They will actually have a shot at graduating high school and entering the mainstream economy—something that their parents were not able to achieve.

So if the national discussion about gentrification is not about financial flourishing, then what is it about?

According to David Doig, "It's nuanced. I'm thinking of our experience in Pullman. Before we started, this neighborhood was 90 percent African American. Now it's 92 percent African American. We have a high number of college-educated people, and we are not seeing wholesale displacement. At all. I'm not sure why the media is so fixated. It might be partly about culture. There is a generational issue: Millennials who are philosophically more progressive feel that housing is a fundamental right. I don't disagree with that, but taken to its extreme, it produces a sense of entitlement to live anywhere they want at a price that's affordable for them."

My conversation with David was leaving me itching to achieve the positive outcomes that David lives every day.

"How is it going for you?" he asked as we wrapped up.

"Lousy! I have *no* support from the city government, and our one existing affordable housing builder has pulled out completely. I mean, if you gave me $400 million I could build something cool too. How in the world would I marshal those kinds of resources without city support?"

The answer to my last question, David and I agreed, would come down to three things. First, you need a big area with a strong anchor institution so that you can achieve scale. Second, you have to be good at collaboration so that you can pull the public and private sectors together. Third, you need to fund strategically, by creatively using both free-market vehicles and government vehicles.

The Sunrise Center showed me that place matters, and that once I have a place, all sorts of activities can occur that positively impact people's upstream health. I saw that when this idea is applied at a huge scale, the impact is even bigger. I could see that developing this principle further might be my future. But what I didn't see coming was that the system that I threatened was gearing up to hit back, and hit back hard. It was a brutal takedown that I barely survived.

CHAPTER 9

Let's Part Friends

*G*resham's assistant city manager smiled and said, "What we are trying to say, Brad, is let's part friends."

"Friends?" I asked incredulously. "What do you mean, *friends*? You don't know what you are asking. You want me to abandon the Sunrise Center, shut down the CDC, lose my livelihood, eat $84,000, and break my covenant with Oregon's poorest community! Is that it? Over what, exactly?"

I had not seen this attack coming. I had been working through a dispute with the city's urban renewal department over some unpaid property taxes, but that issue had been around for over a year, and we were managing it together toward a good resolution. When the city manager's office called me to set up a meeting, I expected a routine meeting to provide an update on this tax issue. But when Lynn and

I walked in, there sat the city's attorney, the urban renewal director, his admin, the city manager, and the assistant manager. It was a setup. The mood at city hall had become threatening overnight.

For the next thirty minutes, the Gresham team laid out their indictment against us, focusing on the unpaid property taxes. The Sunrise Center should have been almost tax-free, but one year a $17,000 mistake had been made by the county assessor's office, and I was in the process of trying to fix it. In a different year, there had been a different $17,000 mistake, and that one had been mine. Because the city owned the Sunrise Center, they had already paid the $34,000 to the county on my behalf, and now they wanted an immediate payment from me for all of it.

What was behind this sudden crisis? Was the city cash poor? I knew that the city had about $50 million in cash and investments on hand, so that wasn't it. I knew that they didn't want to run the Sunrise Center themselves, so that wasn't it either. I enjoyed excellent professional relationships with Gresham's rank-and-file staff. And I wasn't aware of anyone from the community of Gresham complaining about us, except the usual nonprofit leaders who wanted us out of the building so that they could have it. What a curious thing that this kind of roadblock should appear just as the Rockwood CDC was starting to change the city-wide conversation toward a more equitable future for everyone.

"I need for you to tell me what this is really about," I said. "If I can understand the city's needs better, then I can work with you to meet those needs. But I won't just walk away from my commitments because you want to part friends."

In addition to the $34,000 in back taxes, I owed $50,000 to the former owner of the building that housed the Sunrise Center because, after the city agreed to buy it, they didn't actually close on it for three months. That delay meant that, unwittingly, I became a user of the building who did not have an active lease. My lease with the former owner of the building spelled out that, if I were ever in that position, I would owe him *$14,000* per month, rather than the $7,000 of my original deal. No one from the city told me that they hadn't closed on time, so when the former owner presented me with a $50,000 bill, I was shocked. I tried to get the city to pay it, since it was their fault, but they refused to own up to their responsibility. I worked out with the former owner a payment plan of $2,000 per month for twenty-five months. One feature of this payment plan was that if the Rockwood CDC failed to pay it, I would personally pay it. So I was on the hook for $50,000. The only source available to me for the money to repay what I owed was the Sunrise Center itself. If Lynn and I walked away from it, as the city of Gresham was requesting, then we would have no means to retire this debt. We *had* to keep running the center.

The city attorney was happy to wield the hammer. "You need to retire this $34,000 property tax bill in the next nine days," he said, "or we will declare you in default on your lease and evict you."

They didn't appear to care that I would be stuck with the $50,000 debt. They didn't care that the center was the source of employment for Lynn and me. Not once during the meeting did the city people mention Rockwood, its people or their aspirations, or how important the Sunrise Center had become to the community.

"Okay," I said, "so I have nine days to raise $34,000. Is that it? I can take on that challenge. I mean, hundreds of people use the center every week. I think that if we mounted a Save the Sunrise Center campaign, a lot of people would be glad to help us fight. I'm sure the newspaper would jump on this story."

Apparently they hadn't expected me to play that card. The city manager leaned over to the attorney and said, "All of this over $34,000? Isn't there something we could do?"

Aha. There was their weakness. A fear of bad publicity. Having the mask ripped off. Being shown to be not just irrelevant to the real needs of one-third of their citizens, but actually hostile to them.

"Mr. City Manager, if you were to wipe away the debt and keep our lease, then I would be willing to forgive this meeting."

The city attorney responded for him. "No, we want you out."

"Okay, then we all have nine days to see what happens."

Lynn had the last word. "Regardless of how this turns out, from now on we will establish new ground rules with you. First, we will not attend meetings that have no agenda and no list of invitees made known to us before the meeting. Second, we are ready to reconcile with you anytime, because it's for the good of the people of Rockwood. Just ask tomorrow, next month, or five years from now, and the answer will be yes. But that reconciliation has to have the mayor involved, and there must be a professional mediator who guides us through a restoration process. Nothing less will do because the power imbalance between you and us is too great. You are not safe." And with that, we stood and walked out of the room.

On the car ride home, Lynn and I discussed the surprise attack.

"You know, we are either a part of something great," she said, "or this whole thing is just a huge waste of our lives."

"Well, then I need to tell you what's been happening with the Sunrise Development lately. Ed has been ripping into me. In retrospect, I can see that he knew all about Gresham's surprise attack in advance."

"What do you mean?"

"Someone must have told him—before they told us. I know that the mayor is a close personal friend of his. They hang out together in Palm Springs every February. He's been telling me that I am *hated* by *everyone* in Gresham. And that I should vacate the Sunrise Center immediately."

"What? What about the 1,500 meals that we prepare and serve to hungry preschoolers every week?"

"Doesn't care. He told me that the mayor said, 'If Brad doesn't give up on Rockwood and the Sunrise Center immediately, there will be consequences' I just don't get it. Ed, my own partner, wants me out of Sunrise Development too. In fact, he told me to give up my one-third ownership. None of this makes any sense. There must be something—or someone—behind all of this."

The simultaneous attack by Gresham on one side and Ed on the other got under my skin. Going into that weekend, I could see five years of sacrifice and dreams falling apart. I had always known that community transformation wasn't risk-free, that charging into the breach would be costly. But here I was, financially broke and emotionally fragile, being told by my partner that I should "go dark" until everything blows over. I was so tempted to cave. Fighting the battle of transforming Rockwood, up until now, had frequently been a terrible and joyless trudge through gloom, doubt, deep fatigue, and fear. But now it was becoming an actual threat. We needed $34,000 in nine days, and our previous nine-day record was one-third of that.

That night, I sat on an old oil drum in back of my house and watched the sun set over the fields. Until that day, I had thought that the power and money elite were harmless. They were set up for a massive windfall as Rockwood transformed, so they could be relied upon (I thought) to let me transform it. I had thought them merely cynical—but this was something darker and more calculated. Sorting through my memory, I began to piece together patterns I had never recognized before:

I remembered that in the last budget cycle, the urban renewal agency budgeted $1,000,000 for capital improvements for the Sunrise Center. We didn't need any capital improvements, and when I asked what that was for, I never got an answer. The only way to spend *that* kind of money would have been to tear it down and redevelop the site.

I remembered that Ed had just asked to be released from his noncompete agreement with Sunrise Development so that he would be freed up to build in Rockwood without me. And that he was close friends with the mayor . . . and that he knew about our persecution before it happened.

Then I thought about my conversations with a city staffer who was working on a new housing policy. He had sought me out for help in drafting it, but when he learned that I thought the existing policy was racist, he pulled back.

Then I thought about a recent nasty guest editorial that the local paper, *The Gresham Outlook*, published. Written by D.L. Mayfield, it had called me out by name for building "400 units . . . which will no doubt raise prices everywhere" and calling it "egregious," "morally and ethically wrong," and "profiting off of exploiting." (That we were building just forty units at below-market prices and not four hundred market-rate units apparently didn't register with the paper when they ran the editorial.)

Then I remembered that the chair of my board of directors, a banker, told me that I had gotten too close to entrenched interests and that she could not personally afford to be viewed as a threat to them. She had resigned that week.

I went back in and sat at the kitchen table. "Lynn, what if this isn't about us at all? What if this is about tearing down this old building and replacing it with a twenty-million-dollar building with high-priced apartments? And what if the person they want to build it is none other than my partner? And what if he is secretly hatching this scheme with the mayor?"

While I was still mulling this over, my phone chimed with a text message from a local reporter requesting an interview. "I heard about you stealing money from the city of Gresham. That Gresham wants you out. Do you care to comment?"

"No," I texted back, "I am not going to give you an interview, and how did you learn about the conflict with Gresham anyway? I didn't even tell my staff yet."

I spent a hard weekend staring into the abyss of systemic evil. On Sunday, I ran into a friend who led a major nonprofit in Oregon and who had recently run into a very similar wall. He described the backbiting, the illegal maneuvers, and the lack of awareness by rank-and-file citizens. It amazed me. He described it as the toughest battle of his life because the bad players were so well concealed.

If his story and my story were taking place at the same time in just the Portland area, were there more? A quick Google search revealed a resounding yes. I had thought that my middle-class innocence had already been stripped away—now I was learning just how much I still misunderstood. I was learning that any community transformation effort cutting to the heart of the matter should expect to be blasted the moment it crosses the invisible line. On one side of the line is bemused tolerance by the vested interests. On the other side is a brutal takedown and silencing.

"Lynn—the government, our partner, the media, and even a couple members of our own board came against us all at the same time. Have we made a giant mistake? Is it responsible of us to lead our vulnerable neighbors—and our vulnerable selves—into a brick wall? And the scary thing is that I don't see the neighborhood getting any better because of us anyway. Maybe we *should* just move on with our lives."

What did I mean about the neighborhood not getting any better? Just this: Rockwood had actually become a poorer community since I started. Not a richer one, not more successful—poorer. Things were actually going worse for our neighbors. I had thought that as the economy recovered from the Great

Recession, Rockwood would too. But the numbers were moving in the wrong direction. In 2008, the difference between the average income in Multnomah County and the average income in Rockwood had been 35 percent—meaning that the average wage earner in Rockwood made 35 percent less than the average wage earner in the rest of the county. Instead, the recovery has helped everyone else but not us. Incomes were way up in the county. But in Rockwood, not only had they not risen; they had actually declined, and the gap now was 50 percent.

I recalled a conversation I had recently with a woman visiting Rockwood. She does relief work in a refugee camp in Sudan. After checking out the homeless family shelter in Rockwood, run by the county, she was shocked. "Our refugee camps in Sudan aren't as bad as this shelter," she said.

I was also thinking about neighborhood unrest. In part because of my efforts, neighbors had been testifying at city council meetings, expressing their fears. Apartment prices were rising, incomes were dropping, and there was no humane housing policy for people who wanted to stay in Rockwood. My neighbors were now seeing for themselves the hardness of the larger community toward the poor—and the widespread belief that the best thing for the rest of the community is for the poor to be wiped out by inevitable gentrification. At those city council meetings, Rockwood's residents were being rejected and resisted.

I was thinking about my Latino neighbors, who had been worried for the past several months. Alarmed about ICE illegally rounding people up in this neighborhood, Latinos in Rockwood were avoiding the public sphere. Latino churches were seeing declines in attendance. At the Sunrise Center, where previously Latinos had been heavily involved, they were now nowhere to be seen.

And I was thinking about organizations with resources they could bring to this community who were saying, "We're rethinking

Rockwood right now. Maybe this isn't a solvable problem." And a supporter who lives in the rich part of town who said, "You know, at the end of the day, this isn't my community. I'm not sure why I'm working so hard to solve problems on the other side of the metro area."

Maybe I *was* delusional after all. Any normal person would have quit before things got any worse. But I was not normal. For just three years earlier, I had been changed forever when, in the Philippines, I held a dying child.

———

As CEO of a major NGO in the Philippines before my work in Rockwood, I would visit remote villages to assess our work there. We traveled to those villages in a series of vans, complete with staff and cameras—quite a roadshow. I visited dozens of villages around the country, and most of them were similar. One, though, was different in that half the huts were built on legs about four feet off the ground, and there were gangplanks that connected them all. When I asked why, I was told that a few years before, half the village had been forced off the land by the owner, so they built over the ocean. When the tide was out, as it was when I was there, people could walk on the ground below their homes. And when it was in, they walked on the gangplanks and platforms above. Small children regularly fell off these gangplanks, and sometimes one would drown.

It boggled my Western mind that people lived like this. I couldn't help feeling that there was a difference between poverty and, well, stupidity. I mean, how could this way of life be the most rational and practical choice for these particular people? How did this make sense, even by Filipino ultrapoor standards? When even their *neighbors* shook their heads in disbelief, then what was *I* supposed to think?

I'll tell you what I *did* think. I thought that below—*way* below—ultrapoverty, there is something else. Something more profound. But I could not put a name to it until later.

———

Touring a village like this always seemed like a scripted affair. My staff had worked out the logistics and always paid careful attention to social protocols.

"Look over here, but not over there."

"Come meet this lady. She has a successful small business. But don't talk to *that* lady."

There seemed to be a narrative, a script, and I was both the audience and one of the players. Local leaders knew that they could lead this white American executive around by the nose and influence him toward conclusions that, back at headquarters, would cause new resources to flow their way. And there is nothing wrong with that. Their very survival might be at stake.

So on that particular day, the lead staffer was mortified when I went off-script. She had mentioned that a shack a mere ten feet away contained a profound child neglect case, and that my organization's resources could prevent this from happening again. In all of my previous tours of villages, I would simply note the input and say something like, "Oh, I'm sorry to hear it," and move on. There was, after all, a schedule to keep. But the proximity of the problem changed things for me this time. Just ten feet away . . . I knew that I needed to engage with this story right now.

"I want to go inside."

"Sir, I don't think—"

"We are going inside."

All of the little huts in the village were the same. They were made of wreckage. There is a logic to the building materials: If your hut is made of wreckage, and a hurricane tears it down, you can rebuild it out of wreckage. Because there were no windows and no electricity, the huts were surprisingly hot and dark inside. When I entered the hut, I had to stand for a moment to let my eyes adjust because of the contrast between the vivid tropical sun and the deep darkness inside the huts. When I could finally see, there was, of course, nowhere to sit because people there do not have furniture. My organization ran eighty-five preschools, and on the first day of school, the children were taught what a table and chair are. For many of these four-year-olds, it was the first time in their lives that they sat at a table of any kind.

In this shack, I sat where everyone else sat. The dirt.

Through an interpreter, I learned about Joshua. Joshua's father left to drive a jeepney in Manila and has never returned. His mother died of tuberculosis. The government worker brought infant Joshua to his next of kin, his mother's sister. This aunt tried to refuse him, because she herself was malnourished and could not feed the kids she already had. But the worker left him with her anyway, and she was forced to add Joshua to her long list of problems.

"Where is this boy?" I asked.

"He is there, sir." I peered into the shadows and saw a child of perhaps eight or nine.

"Come here, son," I said. Joshua's aunt shifted uncomfortably.

Joshua began to move, but not on his feet. He scooted along on his filthy rear. As he came closer in the dim light, I could that he had big brown eyes and that he was short, all bony angles.

"What is wrong with him?"

"No one knows, sir."

"Has he seen a doctor? Why doesn't he walk? Or speak?"

"Sir, no one talked to him, so he does not talk. The other children will not touch him. He eats scraps if the family has any."

"So, it's possible that he is of normal intelligence, but lacks development because he has been completely neglected?" I asked incredulously. "He just, what—lies in the corner year after year?"

"Yes, sir."

I looked at the faces of the adults in the hut and those peering in from the outside. I could not comprehend this level of neglect. My staff photographer wanted the shot, but I glared him away.

Turning to the boy, I felt something well up inside me that I hadn't felt before. Although he was diseased and reeked of feces, I brought Joshua up onto my lap. I held him. He was so soft. I stroked his hair, and he closed his eyes. There was for me a profound moment of silence.

How powerful is the grip of poverty on this household that no one taught this boy how to walk? To speak? It is the most natural thing in humans to encourage a toddler. But in Joshua's case, no one cared enough to hold out their arms and coax him to come to them. He never heard his name spoken or had anyone respond to his cries. He was by the time I met him that day, so developmentally delayed that there would be no catching up. There would be no diagnosis or treatment. He would die young. I'd be surprised if he were still alive as I write this.

Joshua was past the breakdown and the mourning, and now it was time just for mercy. I held him until I couldn't, and then set him back on the floor. I rose to my feet and left the shack. My staff and the neighbors were silent.

I spent the evening alone. I collapsed in the shower. I threw away my pants. I fell asleep early.

I called Kiesel the next day to tell him about Joshua. I couldn't find the word that described what lay just below ultrapoverty, the thing that made it so damn mean.

"Evil," he said instantly. "What you experienced was evil. Not like in a horror movie. It's more basic than that. It waits and drains.

It gnaws. It has no purpose. It never redeems the sufferer. It's only about destruction. It's evil."

We don't talk about *evil* in the US anymore, but I instantly saw that Kiesel was right. Cradling a neglected and dying boy didn't make me sad, or depressed, or angry. It just emptied me. Kiesel continued: "Understand that the power brokers in Washington, DC and Singapore and Brussels who control Poverty, Inc. do not understand this. At all. They think that they understand, but they do not. They can't see Joshua now or ever, because what they need to see in order to do their jobs are the assets in the communities that are efficient and effective. Joshua is neither. He offers *nothing*. Except for the funding that is tied to headcount, he has no value whatsoever."

I got it. I was CEO of a major multinational nonprofit, and I knew that there was nothing Joshua could provide me except his presence. My commitment to self-preservation and to self-dealing, both personally and professionally, was of no interest to this boy who could offer me zilch. I wondered: Is it true that everyone has a purpose? That everyone has an intrinsic value just because they exist? I mean, if nobody wants to buy anything that I make, or read anything that I write, or eat anything that I cook, then of what value am I?

Hopelessness, purposelessness, valuelessness. No one is known by these descriptors, because when one is in these states, one is not known at all. Maybe someone has value because his headcount drives revenues for a nonprofit. If that is true of Joshua, then he is not marked by what he produces, but by what he receives. Would I ever want to be known solely as someone who has been the grateful beneficiary of the lavish gifts of strangers?

But fortunately, as a white, middle- to upper-middle-class man, I will never have to live with purposelessness for long. My social capital is so great that I can figure out a way to get back in control of my life, and to get back in control of assets that will produce wealth. I can rev back up the hope machine and skitter away from the boundary of valuelessness. And I can go back to ignoring the pain inside me and all around me.

Kiesel spoke again. "So this is escapable for you. You'll move on, and Joshua will stay in his dark hole. Is that it? Is that okay? Or is there more?"

No, it was not okay, and that wasn't it, and there is more. I finally saw that, as the CEO, I had a responsibility to remind my team and my staff that every number is a soul. I must stay vigilant to the danger posed by objectifying the people we serve, because this is where evil leaks in. I must start a clear conversation around paternalism and power imbalances, and keep it going after I was tired of it. I must drive all of our activities to be *with* our neighbors and not just *for* our clients. I must keep at the very core of the organization the idea that each one of us, from the top to the bottom, must be engaged in proximity to each other and to those we serve—and that this engagement must be vulnerable and empathetic. At risk if I fail is this stark reality: I, too, could end up leading Poverty, Inc.

So there it was. Things were not as simple as I'd thought. Joshua was unable to escape his world, and I was unable to escape mine. Both of us were—and still are and will be—captives of a global system of efficiency, effectiveness, and utility. My life during this time had focused on understanding the "how" of human flourishing. While this is a good pursuit, it does not even come close to the real issue, which is much bigger than the question of how to promote flourishing, or how we as a global society should organize ourselves. In the last hundred years or so, our world has decided that if an individual human life has no utility, then it has no value. And we have decided that the value of my life is *also* measured against its utility. Let's just pause for a moment and acknowledge this fact. Let's mourn the death of intrinsic human value, and also the powerlessness that any one of us has to restore it. Let's pray that the only One who can redeem this will redeem it soon.

And having acknowledged that, let's pick up our tools and go to work building what we can to restore human dignity and worth.

———

A year later I was back in the US and launching the Rockwood Community Development Corporation of Oregon under the brand name Rockwood CDC. A good organization knows its core values, and I knew that I had to honor Joshua. I termed one of our four core values "It's Personal." *It's Personal* means that no one at the RCDC gets to solely work behind a desk in an office and call themselves engaged. Everyone must be involved personally in the life of a low-income neighbor in one way or another. Of course, many of our staff are themselves low-income neighbors, so we have not had much trouble enforcing this value.

This is why, when Gresham wanted Lynn and I to walk away, I found that I could not walk away from Joshua.

That Sunday night I arranged a conference call with a few close friends, including Pastor Jason, who had stepped up financially to help me create the Rockwood CDC in the first place. Jason had been thinking a lot about a story in the Bible that relates to my journey. In that story, the main character had returned to his city to rebuild it, just as I did. He engaged his neighbors in the work, just as Lynn did. And he endured threats from entrenched interests who did not want him to finish building the security wall around his city. The pressure on him was great, and he wanted to quit too. But he persevered. And the city was saved.

"Brad and Lynn, I am saying this as intensely and truly as I know how," Jason said. "Stand firm on the ground that you have taken. Your authority comes from your commitment. Do. Not.

Climb. Off. Your. Wall." Lynn and I both needed to hear that. It was more than just encouragement. It was an authoritative charge, a consecration, to stay true in our fight. I saw absolutely no way that I could be saved from complete financial and relational ruin in the week that remained before our deadline, but standing before Jason that night, I committed to doing everything I could to stave it off.

On Monday morning, I decided to let everyone in our broader circle know that we had a crisis, and that we were going to treat the crisis with the same sense of open hands that we had every one of our previous crises. No holding back. Everyone needs to rally. I reached out to the Chairperson of Multnomah County, someone supportive of our work who could possibly influence that $17,000 property tax bill, due only because of an error on the county's part. My voicemail was urgent and direct. She didn't call back, but on Wednesday I called the Assessor's Office to get an exact amount owed, and the representative said, "There must be some mistake. We don't show an open amount for that year. You owe us nothing."

Your authority comes from your commitment.

Whoa. Halfway there. Thank you, Chair Kafoury.

On Tuesday, a donor who, until then, usually gave about $1,000 per year, asked to hear all about my crisis. We met, and after hearing me out, she pulled out her checkbook. "My accountant just told me that I need to donate more out of my charitable trust," she said—and wrote a check for $16,000. Others pitched in a few thousand more. We made it—in just forty-eight hours!

On Wednesday, I presented the city of Gresham a check for $17,000 and memoed them that the other $17,000 "never existed," and thus the $34,000 obligation was retired. No one from the city responded—not then, not afterward, or even to this day. They just stopped harassing me. But in contrast, everyone in my world was thrilled. Elated. Proud.

Everyone, that is, except one person.

Ed erupted in anger. "Listen—you can't just pay off your bills and pretend that everything is fine! I want you *gone*. The mayor wants you *gone*. You have no idea how deeply you are hated in this town."

His rant went on and on. "You thought that our little kumbaya project was going to give away apartments to people. That's not what this is about anymore. This is about raw capitalism from here on out." His shaming and bullying were so over-the-top that I wondered if I was watching a piece of theater written by someone not in the room. But I was bulletproof. We had already survived this well-thought-out and coordinated attempt to kill us.

In the weeks that followed, it felt as if the resistance was crumbling. The newspaper that had run the scathing editorial against me ran a new one in support of Rockwood transformation. New donors came on board, and new businesses signed on to our incubator kitchen. Oregon's secretary of state sought us out to celebrate us. Our legal clinic had a breakthrough, our Shalom network grew, and a couple of Speaks! sessions were memorably powerful. Although it took me a long time to get past the raw discomfort of what I'd experienced, I knew that deep down we had broken the back of the opposition and that my next move was to regain momentum. But what would that look like?

I was sharing this dramatic turn of events with Dr. Andrew Marin, from whom I'd first learned about the four core values. Before Andy worked for the White House and the UN, he founded and ran his own community development project in Chicago. His work had also struggled for years before suddenly having its breakthrough.

"When you get a big enough groundswell, when there's enough community momentum behind it, then whether the government has been a part of it or not, not only are they going to change the policy, but they will ask you to help write the new policy. This is exactly what happened to me, including being invited to the White House in 2012 to work on national policy.

"In the beginning, when we were gaining just a little momentum, people began saying to me, 'You should go to the mayor's office,' or 'The Halstead Merchants Association will be excited,' or 'Your alderman really needs to get on board with this.'

"So I went and talked to them. I didn't have any trouble getting meetings. Everyone wanted to hear. But when I told them what was going on, they would literally laugh in my face. Laughing out loud, saying, 'That's impossible.'

"And each time, I would say, 'You can't tell me it's impossible, because it's already happening.' And person after person would send me on my way, from the mayor's office all the way down to a local store owner or pastor. I kept saying, 'Just show up. Just come and see.' But none of the people with titles would. And after they'd laughed me out of our first meeting, they weren't willing to schedule more time. The door was shut. And what was it that horrified them so much? Our efforts to build bridges.

"Clearly, nobody of influence was going to help us. We would have to do it with the neighborhood, with the left and the right, with people who had no influence but did have a commitment to see a better neighborhood and city. All of that changed, of course, when a major shift got underway because so many people believed in our four principles. Then it was like an unstoppable locomotive. And everyone wanted on board."

What Andy was saying resonated deeply with me because of my previous exposure to the optimistic, can-do countries of the developing world. I was surprised how creative and confident those cultures felt, in comparison to the US. Global poverty is on the run, and that is not by accident. We have learned how to use a combination of capitalism and aid to alleviate poverty. In the Philippines, the percentage of people in poverty has dropped steadily and quickly, until now only about 15 percent of the country is below the poverty line—about the same as the US.

In the Philippines, there was a national sense—visible in the media, overheard at cocktail parties, experienced by the poor themselves—that the elimination of unnecessary human suffering was occurring right before their eyes. Their economy is growing twice as fast as ours, and the poor are disproportionally benefitting from this immense change. The Philippines, like almost all of the other "developing" countries, is much more developed than I thought it was. They are proud of this national accomplishment and are puzzled that a similar ethos is not evident everywhere. I wondered if someday, the US could regain this attitude of "can-do" and alleviate the unnecessary suffering within our borders. I could see for myself that the optimism of international poverty-alleviation efforts stands in stark contrast to the pessimism of our domestic fight.

"So the first thing," Andy continued, "is that you get laughed at, followed by a wave of success on the ground, in the communities. Then comes the second thing—you keep in touch with the politicians as much as you can."

"That's a tough one," I said. "They're so cynical and fearful."

"Not all of them. Eventually, influential people get on board, and they have the ear of other influential people. At some point, if you're doing good in your local neighborhood and make a significant impact, and if change is sustainable, then people will notice. And they'll tell others."

"And after that?"

"We had so much on-the-ground representation from people whose lives were bettered that the media started to pay attention. I let the community speak for us. Whenever the media was in the neighborhood—even muckrakers trying to find dirt on us—or when a public figure or influential person came, people from the neighborhood would give nothing but love and go on the record in support of our impact. We got cover stories on newspapers, magazines, TV—everything. I didn't seek out any of it."

"Everyone says that our systems don't work," I said. "But now that I'm six years into this, I disagree. The systems of law, policy, investment, and justice work exactly as designed to benefit the rich and powerful. The soft systems of power and control work because, in part, the poor do not know how they really work. Until suddenly it becomes plain to everyone, and the exposure is glaring."

"Yup. We stayed focused on solutions, on ways to get around the roadblocks. We made ourselves so relevant that we couldn't be ignored or pushed away. Relevancy for me didn't have anything to do with following the latest trend and everything to do with making ourselves so invaluable to a particular need that we *are* the option, even if we are the last option. What I learned over those fourteen years, especially with regard to the government, is that if we get a sufficient wave of commitment and support from the community we're seeking to serve, if they're trying to help us figure out a way forward, then it's not in the best interests of the people in power not to work with us. They need to figure out a way forward *with* us. That's how we got our influence. When the powerful began to see that they were hurting themselves when they pushed us away because so many people across both sides of the divide believed in us and had our back—that was *the* significant turning point that turned us from a little nonprofit to a powerhouse with international impact."

———

A few weeks later I was describing for Willie how we'd won our showdown with the city and what Andy had said about what lay in store in our future. "You know what surprises me about all this?" Willie said. "I didn't know that you *could* say no to the city. You just dug in when they wanted you gone, and they sulked off. I thought that you were done for. I didn't know that people could win these wars."

I felt like a guy in the third act of an action movie. In the second act, he survives a shootout and realizes that even though he's beat up, he will heal, and that his nasty enemy couldn't kill him after all. Then in the third act, he fearlessly goes against the bad guy and wins. Freedom from fear gives unimagined strength. My fatigue and sadness in the early stages of my conflict with the city suggested that I hunker down and adopt a conservative posture, but I knew that I should put my foot on the gas. That community building mainly benefits everyone but me is not a flaw. It's the key to unlocking shalom. Giving even as I am grieving is what this work *is*. This is not a "victim" statement. It is a statement from

Freedom from fear gives unimagined strength.

the most powerful ground that anyone could be standing on. Fresh from staring down my doom and still being okay, I knew deep down that it was time to seize the initiative. It was finally time to declare that what comes next does not resemble what came before. It was sledgehammer time.

I was ready to change the game: to link big money and resources to this community-based work. In 2017 some federal legislation produced a new investment tool: opportunity zone. I had been waiting for such a game-changing opening for six years. I met with my board, and together we decided to form Oregon Community Capital as a new wholly owned subsidiary that would do nothing but raise opportunity zone-related capital and invest it in Oregon's poorest communities, starting with Rockwood. I was so excited about its potential to bring fresh capital that I held the state's first conference to promote the benefits of opportunity zone investing. I shared my enthusiasm with my district's representative to congress, but he told me flat out that he would try to get the legislation overturned. As we talked, I understood the reason for his opposition: This breakthrough way of helping poor communities would not bring new revenue to the government immediately, and there was no mechanism whereby the bureaucrats could control the investments.

"Brad, this is going to let bad people do bad things to the poor communities," he said.

"Yes. That will happen. But there is also no reason that good people can't use it to do good things with our poor communities. Go knock yourself out in Washington to maintain the status quo. I'm going to knock myself out in Oregon to bring hope."

> **It eventually dawned on me that my organization was bigger than the local government.**

Governmental people tend to think that government alone can solve our problems. But I had a different perspective—one that I developed in one of the most remote parts of the world. On the far southern island of Palawan, my staff would meet with the local governmental staff to review cases of individual child malnourishment or neglect. The two teams were seamlessly integrated, handed over files to each other, and discussed interventions. As I watched the interaction, I saw over and over that most of the action items were taken by my team. Wasn't it the government's responsibility to care for these kids, and my team's responsibility to lend a helping hand? But my organization had a larger staff, more disposable cash, and more professional expertise than local government did. This was a big disconnect for me as an American, where the federal, state, and local governments are so huge. They dominate our communities by their sheer size, and as a result I reflexively wait for them to do something. When they don't, I criticize and blame them. But when I considered that in any American city or suburb, the combined size of the social, educational, and religious sectors is in reality larger than the government, I realized that I needed to adjust my perspective. A combination of these sectors could, and perhaps should, drive the agenda in a community.

Where does that leave the government? With a responsibility to help and to support. I caught a vision of what it might look like to flip the script and reassert the rightful leading role of citizens in solving their own problems. This insight into what is possible would play a big role when I returned to the US to chart a new course for local communities.

Filled with resolve, with Oregon Community Capital firmly in place, I looked forward to the future for the first time in a long time. I don't know if there is a word for what I felt, but it is somewhere at the intersection of gratified, solemn, anticipatory, sad, and special.

I found out only later what a surge of change had been unleashed.

CHAPTER 10

The Dam Breaks

In the middle of a muggy July night in 2020, Vince Jones-Dixon sat up in bed and cried. It wasn't the first time this vibrant young African American man wept. In 2013, Vince's world had been ripped apart when his brother, Dre, was murdered in a parking lot across the street from my office in Rockwood. It had happened on a warm June day, and I had heard the gunshots through my open door.

The murder raised questions that Vince was not able to answer about how his brother descended from a stable family that lived six miles away in a middle-class neighborhood to his death in Rockwood. In 2015, two years after his brother's death, Vince sat in our Lunch and Learn and first learned about this neighborhood, home to drug-related violence. He had become active with us since. He had been the emcee at our candidate's forum—the first that Rockwood had ever had. He cut the ribbon on the dedication of the Sunrise Center. Vince emceed our Opportunity Community programs, and was at every Time to Talk, Time to Listen with the police. Vince had tried to become a Gresham cop himself, but Captain Robin Sells was against him. Then he began to wrestle with the thought that he could change the police from the top if he were a city councilor.

And that's why he awoke crying on that July night—he was wrestling with what he suspected might be a calling, and he was overcome with dread.

Vince's wife awakened and asked him what was wrong. "I *know* that if I won a seat, I could change things," he said. "I could build bridges. The price would be high, because there's so much hate. But if not me, then who? I mean, I can't not."

That was the June of Ferguson, the June of George Floyd. A growing number of African American neighbors were making their voices heard. Vince found the courage to commit to being one of those voices to transform his community. He and others began to put pressure on the city. Even though by this time the CDCO had more Black, indigenous, and people of color in management and on the board than white people, we were still thought of as a white-led organization. So Lynn and I took a backseat and did what we could to encourage the fledgling voices of the community. When one of our partner organizations wanted to hold a George Floyd rally at the Sunrise Center, the answer was *yes*. When Vince wanted me to appear in a campaign video, the answer was *of course*. When those on the city council wanted to talk to a safe person about their fears and concerns, I was glad to do a phone call.

The external pressure on the city was orderly but persistent.

Internally, the city was in complete chaos.

That summer, Police Chief Sells got direct orders from her superior, who was African American, to reform the department to bring their policing methodology into current practice—which left the police department feeling increasingly embattled and threatened. Chief Sells defied those orders. Her superior was getting ready to take legal action against his employer, the city, because of the hostile work environment. And on another front, a Gresham resident (who was a person of color) had alerted the mayor to some policing events that had taken place in Gresham about which the resident was concerned. The Police Department chaplain sent that resident a message with alarming content. The chaplain said that what the resident had done to the chief was "reprehensible" and "will not be forgotten," and that "you have awoken a sleeping giant and that was a fatal flaw to your political career."

But what happened next no one had seen coming. In June Chief Sells suddenly announced her early retirement and left the force. On her way out, she published a letter that made harsh and inaccurate statements about her superior. She called this Black professional "lazy." Dramatic, we all thought—but it got much more dramatic.

The next chunk of the dam that broke was the unexpected early retirement of the city manager. He was the one who'd bought the Sunrise Center and leased it to us, but he was also the man who'd engineered the attempted takedown of our organization over the false charges that we owed the city money. He had weathered many storms over his long career, but all of us could see that this boat was sinking. The culture at city hall of "go along to get along" was being questioned. Its blithe racism was being called out. The unquestioned power of the mayor was suddenly a question. And then it was more than a question. It was a call to action, to reform, to turning over organizational rocks and seeing what crawls out. When I talked to leaders at city hall in those weeks, their responses smelled like fear. I don't know what prompted the city manager's resignation, but one day, after decades of tending the dam that held back the progress of tens of thousands of low-income and non-white citizens, he was gone.

And then the whole thing crumbled. A week after the two major early retirements, Mayor Shane Bemis announced that he, too, was leaving. He didn't mean that he was retiring. Or that he'd be leaving after the upcoming November election. Or that he'd leave in a month or so after a transition period to allow his successor to settle in. He meant that very night. After eighteen years of ironfisted rule, he did not resign to the city council. He did not discuss it with anyone I know, or anyone I have heard from. He just wrote a long and patently false narrative and posted it to Facebook. It read, in part, "Gresham is as noble as any ever ventured, and I am amazingly proud of what we've become." So proud, I guess, that he cleaned out his office that night and has not been heard from since.

As soon as the dam burst, a wave of water rushed in to fill the void. A few days after Shane left, the new city manager opened an investigation into the resignation of the chief of police and the role of discriminatory practices in that resignation. Other people looked into the old city manager's sudden retirement, as well as into the revelation that the city had a $13 million gap in the upcoming budget.

As I write this, investigations are still ongoing, and we've not yet arrived at the complete truth. The chief of police, the city manager, and the mayor, who had together formed an impenetrable wall, were now gone. We filed a Freedom of Information Act (FOIA) Request in order to learn the truths behind some of the schemes and attacks on us, but in violation of law, the city of Gresham has yet to respond. A council member told me that there are so many requests that the city attorney's office simply cannot process them all. The bad guys always overplay their hand. And when they fold, they fold fast.

Willie watched the collapse of the Gresham government with the same wonderment that I did. Like me, Willie had been biding his time until the bad guys left, and now he wondered if it was finally our time to shine. We sat in his office in the kitchen of the Sunrise Center and talked over the events of the day. As we laughed together, we also acknowledged that the city wasn't my only problem. Just because the dam had burst, that didn't automatically mean that our community was ready to work together to seize its future.

Summer 2020 was a raw time, and especially for the African American community. The combination of the George Floyd killing, the economic and personal losses from COVID, and the presidential election stressed them. We non-Blacks called on our own thin reserves of grace and generosity to help them get through it. But our attempts to hold it all together felt like a failure. Some of the dominant African American voices during the summer of 2020 were from the Black Sovereignty camp. Their goals of separation from white society weren't compatible with the CDC's core value of reconciliation, and they pulled out of our work together. Other voices came from the street, angrily demanding cash so that they could meet the basic needs of the very poor young African American families of Rockwood. We supported their goals, but even so, we couldn't do much except be witnesses to their struggle.

Willie, friendly with both camps, resisted their calls to choose sides. He told me that he wondered whether either camp could work with the long-term interests of Rockwood in mind.

Trust is a difficult issue in Rockwood. Because ours is a networked approach to community transformation, and not a transactional approach, it's personal. We grow at the speed of relationships. But not just easy relationships—*trusted* relationships. And it's even harder than that. We grow at the speed of trusted relationships *across multicultural boundaries.*

The key to finding and nurturing these trusted relationships across multicultural boundaries is to find mediators who stand with one foot in both worlds. Once I had reached out to a prominent African American architect to join our board of directors. As we talked about our work and how he might contribute, he said, "I wouldn't join you simply because you asked. Normally, I wouldn't trust you. But in this case, I do—because I trust Willie, and Willie trusts you."

It has been only recently that I have come to appreciate the price that Willie and his wife, Vanessa, have paid in order to serve as a connection between the African American and the white worlds. Now that Willie and I had established a deeper level of trust, I could ask him plainly why he experienced so much friction with the from-the-streets Black groups and with the Sovereignty groups, when all he is trying to do is be an ally in their fight. Willie addressed it with me using the bluntest terms possible:

"Brad, I'm the kitchen manager and Vanessa cleans the building, right?"

"You're so much more than that, Willie. But yes, that's how most people see you."

"To a lot of Black people in Portland, that makes us your house n******."

"Willie, don't say that!"

"But it's true. In their eyes, we're your house n******. And they are the field n*****, and the two of us don't trust each other. Because to the field n******, us folks in the house will tell Massah what's what and who's who."

"So all of these years," I said, "while you have been patiently working away at transforming this community, you've been targeted by your people because you are too close to me? They've been leaving you out of things because they thought that you would tell me, and that I would—what?—try to thwart them?"

"Yes. It has been hard, but I think now that that day is over."

———

When the dam broke in Gresham, it broke in the African American community too. Willie told everyone in that community that they could lean on us, that we are trustworthy. By the end of the summer, the from-the-street Black group that works with young families moved their operations into the Sunrise Center. A Black business professor from Oregon State joined our board. The Black Food Sovereignty Council joined our food collaborative.

Are the deeper, underlying issues regarding African American distrust of whites resolved? No—and most of us in Rockwood seem aware that they may never be. But in the meantime, we can do great work if we work collaboratively for the good of the city. We are now trusted enough, and as it turns out, that's enough.

Once our opposition at the city of Gresham had departed under a cloud, and with strong, trusting relationships established with those who took their places, it seemed that now was our time. But I had one more foe to fight.

After the Sunrise Development fiasco, many months had been going by between meetings. The apartment building, the first of four planned buildings, had finally opened—two years behind schedule and two million dollars over budget. Hundreds of kids from Rockwood now attended the Head Start program that occupied the first floor. Above that, forty-four new units of decent housing for working families were already full. The building was starting to show a positive cash flow, and Ed was working on getting the second building project started.

Ed still wanted me out of the partnership—although, with his close friend no longer in the mayor's office, Ed's tone got more conciliatory. We both got lawyers who helped us arrive at a cash-out offer that I could live with. Finally, after years of drama and frustration, this episode in the development of commercial and residential property was over.

The collapse of the opposition, the boom in affordable housing, and the forging of new trusted multicultural relationships was all good news, of course. Lynn and I were realizing, with a sense of deep satisfaction, that we had accomplished everything that we had set out to do. But despite the wins, the donor dollars were still not flowing. In fact, at the end of 2019, our total revenues were less than in 2018. Lynn got paid her full salary, but I could only manage to pay myself, from that meager cash flow, $27,312 for my work at the CDCO for that entire year. And our funding forecast for 2020 didn't sound any better. Something had to give.

In February 2020, I told the board that I had to leave the organization. Lynn was perfectly capable of running the Sunrise Center and making appeals to donors. The CDC just wasn't financially capable of supporting two of us. The board reluctantly agreed. Several of them wondered why it had taken me so long to throw in the towel.

None of us in the organization foresaw what would happen next. In the next eighteen months, we went from almost closing and not being able to afford my salary to a yearly budget of $13,000,000, which put us in the top 5 percent of all nonprofits in the US.

What none of us had seen coming was COVID.

CHAPTER 11

Together

If you want to go fast, go alone. If you want to go far, go together.
—**African proverb**

As I entered 2020, I raised a glass to those of us who had persevered and won against the people and institutions who'd
plotted our failure. Life was suddenly springing up all around.
Hundreds of our neighbors were now actively working for the transformation of Rockwood.

Then came March 2020, and the COVID pandemic swept in like
a tornado. Our neighbors were hit hard. They were infected at twice
the rate of the rest of the residents of Oregon, and our rates of hospi-
talization and death were also the highest of any neighborhood. We
were the epicenter of the tornado ripping through our state. Other
underinvested communities were impacted too, of course, but what

caught the attention of our statewide health authority was the newly developed ability of our neighbors to deal with the pandemic ourselves.

What made it so apparent that Rockwood was a community with serious assets was the way we had handled emergency food distribution. Right before COVID hit, our fledgling Rockwood Food System Collaborative had finally started to gel, with as many as twelve separate organizations participating in a monthly Zoom call in which they would share their assets, needs, and strategies, just as any well-functioning Speaks! Level 3 group does. When COVID hit, I wondered: Were we far enough along as a group that we could handle our community's response to COVID?

There was only one way to find out. I obtained a commitment for as many as four hundred boxes per week of emergency groceries from the USDA Farmers-to-Families program. It was the *way* that we planned to distribute food that excited state and federal leaders. Instead of lines of cars at the Sunrise Center, we received pallets of food, broke the boxes down into smaller piles, and then gave those piles to smaller, culturally specific organizations which in turn drove the boxes out to distribution points in the neighborhoods. This way we reinforced the tie between these smaller start-ups and the families they serve. We also secured masks and other personal protective equipment for distribution through the same supply chain. When the dust settled, $1,400,000 worth of personal protective equipment went out, and enough groceries to make 467,100 meals! There were exactly zero other organizations in Oregon who had such a deep reach into their marginalized communities in response to the pandemic.

Ricardo is a smiling, can-do Mixtec from Oaxaca who pulled up in his Ford F-350 hauling a fifteen-foot trailer. He is a social entrepreneur backed by no organization or group. He's just a pillar for his community who quietly goes about meeting needs. We loaded him up with supplies and sent him on his way. Two hours later, Mohammed appeared with his SUV to do the same, but by then we were out of food boxes. We still had stacks of fresh greens from the Congolese farmers who were part of our food system collaborative, but otherwise the staples like rice and beans were gone. Everyone felt terrible about leaving the Muslims out—until the familiar roar of Ricardo's truck made conversation difficult. He had actually taken more boxes than he could distribute, so he brought back the balance for someone else. And since Mohammed's SUV was too small for the bounty, Ricardo offered to truck all of the food to Mohammed's apartment complexes for him. An hour later, when they opened the boxes, both of them realized that the ham steaks had to go. Ricardo brought the ham steaks back, and the African American group snapped them up.

The leaders of each ethnic group were so delighted with how it all worked out that the next week they organized themselves from the outset to do it again. Everyone—Muslim, Mixtec, Congolese, and Black—worked together until COVID subsided.

Our success in making a culturally specific supply chain work caught the attention of the Oregon Health Authority. Could our hub-and-spoke distribution model be applied to other outreach projects? Would we be willing to do COVID education? Pay the rents and buy the groceries for people who were in the hospital? Help set up vaccine clinics? Would we open up the Sunrise Center to COVID-impacted street people on snowy nights? Yes. Yes. Yes. Yes. All of a sudden, the Sunrise Center was looking more like a field hospital than a community center, and we could not have been happier. Pallets of supplies filled the event room, then the meeting rooms, and then the hallways. Tents sprang up in the parking lot, and volunteers showed up, their smiles hidden by masks. In a water-bucket line, the Latino leader handed boxes to the Burmese leader, who loaded them into a car heading to a Slavic apartment complex.

Seeing the torrent of money from Washington, DC, that was being released for COVID relief, I started writing grant proposals furiously, sometimes submitting one every two or three days. We won most of them and closed 2020 with revenues 4.2 times what they were in 2019. Of the $2.2 million that came in, 70 percent went out to partner organizations, and 20 percent directly to our neighbors. The 10 percent that we kept paid all of our administrative and overhead expenses, including my own oft-delayed salary.

We were finally able to greenlight the dream that Lynn had had since we'd started eight years before. She created a new unit of the CDCO called East County Community Health. She was now able to hire navigators who could connect people to services, and services to hard-to-reach people. Our staff today speaks twelve languages and comes from all over the world. Because our new staff members were from the displaced groups themselves, they knew where the poverty was hiding. Martina connected us to an immigrant family whose father was in the hospital with COVID. When Martina entered their living room to perform a needs assessment, she counted five children. She learned that in this dingy home, those five kids shared just two pairs of shoes among them. CARES Act funding allowed Martina to immediately buy groceries, pay the rent, and yes, put shoes on those little feet.

One of the delights of launching our new community health unit was the process of hiring its leader. We created the Director of Community Health position and advertised it nationally. Stellar candidates applied because what we are doing, even though it's rarely practiced, is in line with current design philosophies for community health systems. As Lynn progressed through the candidate selection process, one name kept rising to the top: Christine. And indeed, Lynn finally hired Christine because she scored the highest of any candidate. When I met her for a final interview, she looked familiar. And then Lynn reminded me that eight years before, Christine had been the lonely social entrepreneur in the trailer park next to the tracks who was simply serving children. In the years since, Christine had earned two master's degrees and was running a housing program for a local nonprofit. After a national search, here she was—a local who had originally inspired me to create a backbone organization instead of providing direct services. Eight years before, Lynn and I had formed the CDC simply because we wanted to serve her. It took us eight years and four million dollars, but by hiring Christine, we finally got there.

As COVID raged, and rose and fell and rose again, our community health group grew. While they administered over three thousand shots to the most hesitant populations, they also took shots at system change. The CEOs of the largest health systems in Oregon began to tour and learn. They are now seeing that they have misused their power to define who and what is normal and how normalcy is achieved, and are asking the questions that they need to in order to use their power better.

Although we were executing on our promises like mad, one of the questions that kept coming up from federal, state, and philanthropic funders was whether the community could actually handle a large influx of resources if they were given. I understood the question, because for years I'd had it too. I understood their skepticism that a community could build its own capacity to deal with a crisis. For most of my life, I'd viewed low-income neighborhoods through a deficit lens, and not through a capacity lens.

I understood how hard it is to let go of the deficit lens. This middle-aged American still thought about the searing images of starvation in India. When that Asia disappeared, I do not know, but what sits on the same plot of Asian ground now is modern and exciting and young and hopeful and energetic. They are winning the war on poverty. In China, in 1990, two-thirds of the population lived on $1.90 or less. In 2015, it was less than 1 percent. During the same period, infant mortality is down 80 percent, and per capita income is up 900 percent. Africa is where China was in 1990, and they too are solving hunger and poverty fast. This story is not understood in the West, and as a result, most of the folks with dough they want to invest to address poverty are still aiming their resources at problems that simply no longer exist.

We are wrapping up the massive project that is poverty alleviation—eliminating unnecessary human suffering. We need to celebrate it! The most forward-looking organizations see that the curtain is dropping on the final act of this tragedy/success story, and they are preparing for that day.

David Austin has invested his life in "what matters." He is now one of the top managers at the United Nations World Food Programme, and his office is on K Street in Washington, DC—the very seat of power. David is a part of the senior leadership team that figures out how, where, and why to distribute more than seven billion dollars to people every year. When Lynn and I have coffee with him, it's like breathing straight oxygen to get a fact-based line of reasoning that runs completely counter to the fear-based line in the popular media.

Over a latte, David gets right to the point. "The first thing you have to understand about global poverty is that we are winning, and there is an end in sight.

EXTREME POVERTY RATE FROM 1800 TO TODAY

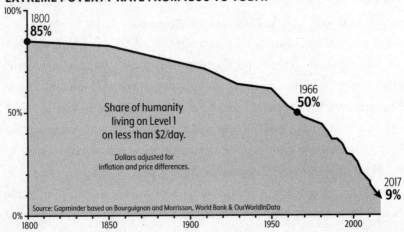

"If you go back to 1800, looking at the whole world, almost everyone lived in extreme poverty. Then by 1966, half the world's population lived in extreme poverty. From 1966 to 1991, just a twenty-five-year period that included agriculture's Green Revolution, poverty dropped to 30 percent. From 1991 to 2017, it dropped to 9 percent. Today, we're probably at 7 percent. By 2030, we hope to end hunger everywhere. We should all be proud of this historic accomplishment.

"And that is even more amazing when you consider that, from 1966 to today, we *doubled* the world's population. By 2100, Africa will have five billion people. The rest of the world—another five billion. They will all be fed, they will all be educated, they will all have health care. They will have access to market economies."

"So if we understand how and when this progress in the fight against poverty and hunger happened," Lynn said, "and what the future trends are, then why is our media full of negative news? I have to admit, I'm having a hard time even processing this. Because if what you are telling me is true, then our role—yours and ours—as the people who run the world's systems combating poverty, may not be needed for much longer. I'm wondering if we'll be ready to let go of that role."

"Don't get ahead of yourself. We'll be needed for another decade or two. But that era is predictably coming to a close."

One troubling pattern, despite this progress, is that much of the aid world, both internationally and domestically, is still defining people by their deficits. They feel as if they are forced to, because more money is raised on people's deficits than on their strengths. When shalom breaks out, relief organizations struggle to find their footing. But in our case, and in this emergency, the folks who wrote big checks were inspired by the newfound capacity of our neighborhood to build on its assets. I believe that slowly and haltingly, other philanthropic, investor, and government sources are increasingly willing to fund the flourishing of distressed neighborhoods.

———

While the horrors of COVID raged, the beauty of our multicultural response to it filled me with hope. We had discovered the structure of belonging that exists just below the surface in every community, and we engaged it to bring lifesaving resources to the most doubtful and disconnected families. The first time I learned to build on community assets was ten years before, when I worked for a large organization in the Philippines. In that country, there was a lot more economic activity among the poor than my organization let on. There were more quality schools and effective churches, more hygiene infrastructure, and more roads and jobs than there had been even a few years before. High-speed data and instant phone contact were reaching further and further into the islands. Filipinos everywhere had deep family ties to expat Filipinos the world over and were increasingly sophisticated about buying and selling in global markets. The "deficit" narrative that we sometimes used to raise donor dollars did not always match the reality on the ground.

I was not the only one growing uncomfortable with the narrative of "deficit" that we were pushing out to donors. My capable Filipino leadership staff were uncomfortable with it too. One day I was walking in a stunningly beautiful mountain pass with one of my base leaders. We were talking about how the growing Filipino middle class could be giving pesos of their own toward poverty alleviation if they were challenged to do so. "Sir Brad," he said as we stared out over the expanse of green and down to the blue ocean below, "how long do we have to be the 'poor Filipino' who needs everything from Europeans and Americans? We are so grateful for their help, for sure. Eternally so. But maybe we would be better off if they let us do for ourselves everything we are capable of. You know, once you build the building, you take away the scaffolding. When does America's scaffolding come down?"

I thought it over. "I'm going to be honest with you," I said. "When I came here, I saw you through the lens of *deficit*. I saw you as a mouth to feed, a foot to be shod, and a mind to educate. But now I see you very differently. What I'm hearing now is about valuing the assets that you already have and building on them. About hearing your hopes and dreams and removing barriers that keep you from realizing them. About respecting your innate desire to be a peer at the table. This is a completely different worldview."

It had been eight years since Lynn and I had started to intervene in our distressed neighborhood, and our long-game strategy of development, rather than relief, was working—and working really well. The social capital that this community now possessed was deployed to massively fight back against COVID. It was no longer just "my" organization. It was now about two dozen organizations, fighting together. Why wasn't everyone on this path?

In an early conversation with Dr. Peter Clark, I had said, "The people who run Poverty, Inc. aren't stupid. Why doesn't everyone give aid with an eye for long-term development?"

Peter thought for a while before answering. "There is still a propensity among the aid organizations for getting the quick bucks. They receive enormous amounts of money, which they feel they need to spend quickly and move on. But it doesn't *have* to be this way. One of the great experiences of my life was working with Tearfund UK. When Hurricane Mitch tore through Central America in 1998, Tearfund got something like fifteen million pounds through a BBC appeal. Their leaders at the top said, 'The Red Cross can distribute food and medicine. We'll work with our partners on the ground who are there long-term to do development work and rebuild.' Tearfund had to stretch their response time to three to five years, but that extra time enabled them to be much more effective."

That made sense to me. Remember the Relief → Betterment → Development continuum? I found myself thinking that just about everyone needs to shift the focus from relief to development.

This idea is summed up in the term *capacity building*. Capacity is built when the local community participates in their growth, when leaders emerge, when every individual has more skills, when there is a shared understanding of the problems that the community faces, when there is a shared vision for the future, when there is a widely understood agenda, when there is tangible progress toward goals, and when effective organizations and institutions can guard the process for the long term. Government's help in capacity building is optional but desirable.

"Peter," I said, "it sounds like the work of capacity building shifts the focus from us—in our case, the Rockwood CDC—to them, in our case, our Rockwood neighbors."

Peter nodded. "If we can work with communities to build capacity, then these communities have a chance to thrive. They can increase their own disaster preparedness. Their government can become more transparent and responsive to the people. They become good stewards of our environment. The local community's success is affected by such things as whether their society is fighting internally, or imploding, or actually flourishing. Those things are beyond the control of donor bodies. Capacity building is truly and profoundly about the capacity of the people to flourish."

With the successful COVID response in place, I turned my attention to boosting our community's capacity to respond to broader issues. I noticed that the state and the county were receiving massive infusions of cash from the feds, but that little of it was making its way to the nonprofits of East Multnomah County. We are 24 percent of the county by head count, and certainly are the poorest. But in the distribution of money, we got just 3 percent. I contacted *The Oregonian*'s venerable columnist Steve Duin, who wrote a piece that called out the inequity. Steve's piece unleashed a firestorm of controversy and ass-covering. People in power could make excuses, but they could not dispute the facts.

Steve's article caught the attention of Oregon's largest philanthropy. They had just received a $65 million allocation from the Oregon legislature so that they could buy hotels and turn them into housing for COVID-impacted families, and then, after the pandemic subsides, for any families needing affordable apartments. Oregon Community Foundation opened a competitive bid process, and all of the usual housing providers made their pitches. I did too, even though up until that point we were not in the club. I described our supply chain of smaller, culturally specific partners and how we could use the same connections to make sure that the most difficult-to-house people were getting housed. To my astonishment, they selected the CDCO for an almost $7 million gift so that we could buy a hotel in Rockwood and put it to use in COVID response. They cited two factors in their decision: one, that with this gift they could start to fix the underinvestment in the community that they had read about, and two, that they could reach people who are not normally reachable.

The mega-gift vaulted us into the top 5 percent of all nonprofits in the US (by budget). Given that most small nonprofits in the US saw their budgets *shrink* as a result of COVID, this result was almost completely unprecedented in the whole nation. But the gift did more than that. It signaled to everyone that we had arrived as a real player in community transformation. The pace of conversations about system change quickened. Bank presidents and federal programs sought us out. Politicians who previously couldn't be bothered started calling me. The US Small Business Administration awarded us a one-million-dollar program for

helping immigrant, refugee women, veteran, and minority entrepreneurs get started. Other communities across Oregon want us
to expand into their neighborhoods. Do you know what particularly attracts their attention? Our group of community health
workers and small nonprofit partners were acting as navigators.
The concept of centering the delivery of resources and services
around navigators—the concept that had taken me to the governor's mansion in search of support, the concept that we had originally tried to launch in healthcare delivery—was finally getting
funded. The model that Lynn had first promoted eight years
before had become mainstream.

——

The other day, during a loud and ambitious meeting of our food
system collaborative, I realized that the last time that I had seen
this kind of rambunctious optimism and confidence was in the
Philippines. It struck me that the "can-do" spirit that has been in
short supply in the US of late was blooming in front of me. With a
smile, I thought of all of the things I'd learned in the past eight years.

I learned that the people of a developing community have assets
of their own. And they have finish lines that do not look like mine.
I learned that we must work *with* them, and not *for* them, so that
they can actually add value to our communities.

I learned to do my compassion on the retail *and* the wholesale level.

I learned to reject "top-down" leadership, and I moved toward
proximity.

I held a dying child and realized that there is an evil in this world
that takes many forms, including keeping food out of the mouths of
kids, putting up roadblocks to economical housing, and elevating
self-preservation above all.

I learned that I can summon the courage to confront evil, and that when I do, it flees.

I learned that governmental help is optional.

I learned that when it comes to international poverty aid, we can take the scaffolding off the building, because it is built now. And that once we can finally see the building, we learn that its architecture is not our own. It is theirs.

If the era of paternalism is ending, then what replaces it? Community, capacity building, and power sharing.

If we aren't doing top-down, then what are we doing? Working with our neighbors to identify assets and use them to build from the bottom up.

If we can no longer control other cultures, then what do we have? A relationship.

If we no longer have to worry about self-protection and self-interest, then what do we have? The possibility of shalom.

If we're not working for their benefit anymore, then what are we doing? We're working *with* them for the benefit of us all.

If the deficits of hunger and poverty are filled, then are we done? No. The future is human flourishing. Human flourishing needs different skills and mindsets—away from the old command and control, and into community development.

———

I stopped in the bustling office today to meet with our leadership team. They are tired but happy with the exhilarating pace of change, at both the neighborhood level and the system level. New community teams are thriving, resistance is in retreat, and hundreds of millions of new dollars are flowing into our area. Scarcity, that hunter that stalks the poor, has moved on. "So what are we still lacking?" Lynn asked me.

I said, "The only scarcity left is one of imagination. Let's flourish. With our partners. With our neighbors. Together."

A Knock at the Door

*I*t has been ten years since Renaldo invaded my world, stripping me of my upper-middle-class innocence. Since that time, I have destroyed the strip club where he got his drugs and have built a new neighborhood. If things had been different back then, maybe he wouldn't have ended up beaten and robbed and dumped in my bushes. Maybe Renaldo would have been flourishing.

Lynn and I can understand being robbed and dumped in the bushes, because the road these ten years has been so rough. But we pursued resilience, we pursued life. In the midst of systemic evil, I think that we managed to avoid PTSD and instead ended up with PTG. You know—Post-Traumatic Growth. Shalom is possible.

A few days ago, a young man volunteered with us. It was his first time ever being in a low-income community, and it shook him. He sent me this email yesterday:

> Brad, you shared so many powerful truths today, I am more than full of things to consider. One such principle that you touched on was the courage necessary to connect with others when life gets uncomfortable. I was very moved (still am) by that notion of courage being the centerpiece in the recipe for right relationship and connectivity, no matter how challenging the course. Thank you.

I am, in one sense, very proud of the fact that Rockwood is unstuck and is well on its way to flourishing. But I am not self-congratulatory. The work of reconciliation, justice, prosperity, and health is an ongoing and unfinished work in American society—and that's true of Rockwood as well.

We continue to work with our neighbors to build new narratives of how to address the biggest problems like houselessness, failing schools, poor health outcomes, poverty, and hopelessness. We are branching out to other communities in Oregon that are beginning their own journeys and offering help to young organizations and leaders. We are knocking on doors and inviting change.

Now you know what can be done, what acting is going to cost you, and the joy that you will reap from your actions. I hope that you, like many others in this story, can't not.

Appendices

Go FISH!

*A*fter nine years of learning and growing, we are starting to work with people from other communities around the US who want to accelerate their transformation. These people have found "their own Calcutta." They have decided to make it their business to promote the flourishing of their zip code. They are excited.

But the road is long and confusing. New community development groups are frequently shocked by what they see once they stop looking at other countries or the dysfunction in Washington, DC and turn their gaze much closer to home. They see that once-in-a-hundred-years economic structural change is upon them. They see that there are no other organizations that can lead the way down a different road because the system is committed to its self-preservation. If their city is like Gresham, there is no affordable housing bureau, community development staff, or people of color in its senior leadership. There are no other community development corporations, housing advocacy groups, churches, or cultural-affinity groups that have the scope or legitimacy to mount a community-wide conversation. They know that without their intervention, their neighborhoods will replay the crushing episodes of the past. With it, the community may chart a safe passage to a multi-income, multiethnic future of human flourishing.

Every city in America has a Rockwood, and every community needs to begin this conversation. The media narrative might be that it is too late to do something, but I disagree. Skepticism that people and communities can change is warranted, but it is definitely overblown. Regret that one didn't start sooner should be dismissed, because, as the old adage says, "The best time to plant a forest was forty years ago. The second best time is now." Systemic change is an uphill climb, but it *is* possible, if not inevitable. If I and my small team could unleash all of this change in Oregon's poorest community against stiff opposition in just nine years, then anyone can.

Community development is now a maturing field that is ready for expansion. From its humble roots in the twentieth century, it has carved out an increasingly large role for itself as the "go-to" for taking on a neighborhood's giants. Enough has been tried, measured, refined, and replicated (both domestically and internationally) that communities no longer have to forge solutions on their own. Big money is more available than ever before. A buffet of tools and techniques that are known to work are easily accessible. The door is wide open to businesspeople, neighbors, institutions, faith communities, health centers, schools and colleges, and yes, government, to imagine a new future together. For leaders who begin their work with open hands, a big table, and a ten-year timeline, the probability of success is much higher than they think. Thus *right now* is a time of great creativity and promise.

As our strategy unfolded over the years, I developed a simple roadmap to the resources that are available in this exciting field of community development. The acronym FISH is an easy way to keep in mind the four intersecting roads on the map. I chose FISH because everyone knows that if you give a man a fish, he eats for a day, but if you teach him to fish, he eats for a lifetime. Well, the same idea works for the broader community too. If you give a community a fish, you feed it for a day. But if you teach a community to fish, you feed it forever.

What does it mean to teach a community to fish? It would mean making sure that enough assets are accessible to everyone, and that the right incentives are in place for people to want to use them. The long-term result is a functioning community, a place where shalom may then naturally develop.

Let's look at this idea in more detail, using the acronym FISH. We can group the hard and the soft capital that communities need like this:

F	I	S	H
Financial	**Intellectual**	**Social**	**Human**
Equity	Know-how	Anchor	Education
Debt	Data	Institutions	Jobs
Bonds		Bonds	Personal Wealth
Grants &		Bridges	Building
Subsidies		Aspirations	Business Support
		Navigators	Health
		Social	Services
		Entrepreneurs	Built Environment
		Social Justice	
		Warriors	
		Faith	
		Communities	
		Integration	
		into the	
		Larger Economy	

FINANCIAL CAPITAL

There must be a strange design flaw in our capital allocation markets, because outside of the urban core, most of America's communities are starved for money. Underinvested places are everywhere, and they all exhibit the same stunting of human flourishing. Even simply *talking* about "place" as an investment category introduces a screwdriver into the gears of this capital allocation machine. Investment theses are usually not developed with place in mind. Investment theses frequently disregard place, and incorrectly assume that all places are created equal. That they are not is becoming increasingly obvious, yet it is tough for investment managers to quantify it. Place-based financing addresses this flaw by saying, right up front, that *place matters*.

Place-based investing points out that the standard valuation formula that any appraiser uses to set the resale value for an apartment or a commercial building references the "capitalization rate" of similar properties in the area. The owner takes the annualized cash income for the property and divides it by the "cap rate" to come up with a sale price. This cap rate has way more weight than any other variable in the price-setting formula. A property owner may sweat over whether to use high-grade finishes in a kitchen, for example, but when it comes time to sell, that beautiful granite countertop will have little to do with the sale price.

So how is the cap rate set? It is set by how much other similar properties have recently sold for. As a result, most of the financial value in a building comes from the zip code that it sits in. And the value of a zip code comes from the flourishing of its people. In other words, a building is just an empty box that holds the shalom of the city. If the community is doing well, then the investment does well. If the community is declining, then so does the investment. The math is the math, and it is not radical or new. What most investment managers frequently miss, though, is that the shalom of a place is not just a fixed variable, but rather something that can be improved. Community development can actually change the cap rate, driving up wealth for everyone all at once. "Extra" expenses like building a childcare center, or supporting a jobs program, are viewed as core to the performance of the asset over time. The idea behind place-based holistic investing is that while the efficiency of capital is likely reduced a bit (if at all) on Year 1, over time the resiliency that it buys boosts the asset at Year 10. The community development industry's long experience with new markets tax credits proves that spending money to build the community does not have to cost much—or anything—more than standard investments, and it delivers superior financial returns.

This is why at our Oregon Community Capital division we put at least one of our neighbors on each investment committee. Remember, development is done *with* our neighbors, and not *for* our neighbors. These investment committee members may not know their way around a balance sheet, but they know their way around the community. These committee members frequently identify ways to boost the performance of a project at little to no cost, because they know what it takes to make life in the project area flourish. If place matters, then spending money to make places matters too.

Place-based investing does not mean that people-based investing is unimportant. It means that place leads and forms the people strategy. Development leads betterment, which in turn reduces the need for relief over time. The East Lake neighborhood revitalization in Atlanta is an example. They put a charter school at the heart of that project because it would attract young families to move back into the area around the school. East Lake started with a place-based strategy, then brought in the charter school and other betterment assets, and then the relief services became more effective.

When a community decides to go FISH, they leverage and build financial assets to do it. They tap into the growing, sophisticated, and largely hidden financial infrastructure that brings debt, grants, bonds, and equity to bear. The financial instruments are grouped in these broad categories:

Debt Investments

Debt is a promise that a borrower makes to a lender to repay a loan with interest at a certain time in the future, as well as an agreement on what happens if they don't. The kinds of debt that community-wide projects need are measured in the millions, tens of millions, or even hundreds of millions of dollars. Why choose to go into debt? Because debt can come in bigger chunks than can equity, bonds, or grants. Banks, and especially the ever-threatened community banks, are frequently a source of debt because they are required by the Community Reinvestment Act to place capital in underinvested communities in order to keep the charter that allows them to stay in business. Savings and loans and mortgage companies also are a source of debt. All three issue mortgages that they can later resell to the federal government's Fannie Mae and Freddie Mac programs, which keep grease in the cogs and supposedly make sure that plenty of cash is available for low-income people who qualify for mortgages. FISHers should be aware, however, that banks are frequently not an honest ally in transforming a community because they are *rarely* hurt when they fail to meet CRA requirements, and also because they are barred from relaxing their underwriting guidelines for a project in a low-income neighborhood. In the last half of the twentieth century, they even tightened their standards when people of color wanted mortgages. Redlining is illegal and is supposed to be a thing of the past, but researchers continue to observe greater rejection rates and higher interest rates to Black and Latino borrowers than to whites.

Community banks are supposed to be more responsive to the needs of underinvested neighborhoods. Portland had a terrific one, Albina Community Bank, which for a number of years brought much-needed liquidity into predominately Black neighborhoods. But over time, their clientele moved to Rockwood and their old branches were no longer involved in the lives of the people who lived in the Numbers. I was excited because Albina had signed a letter of intent (LOI) to open their first remote branch in Rockwood when either the City's new development or my new development opened. Sadly, when Albina was purchased by Beneficial State Bank ("Build Something Beautiful"), one of the first things they did was cancel the LOI. The banks, even the good banks, are frequently unreliable players at the system level in America's Rockwoods.

A less harmful debt source is a community development financial institution (CDFI). There are over 1,400 CDFIs in the US, with more than $100 billion in assets, and their numbers are growing. Many understand place-based investing and have financial products that encourage holistic strategies. I have found that CDFIs are relatively conservative lenders and will likely not have underwriting standards that are much better than the banks. But at least they are shooting straight.

Besides the failure of our banks to execute on their mission, there is the nature of debt itself. Debt is not really on the side of the community in its efforts to develop prosperity. Banks *say* that they are sharing risk, but they really aren't. A less-than-ideal feature of debt in underinvested communities is that lenders never or rarely have to be held accountable—either personally or corporately—for the failure of the borrower to repay.[8] The borrower, on the other hand, is held scrupulously to the terms and conditions of the loan document, and risks catastrophe for violating them. Thus, the amount of risk-sharing that banks actually do is minimal. Of the four elements of financial capital in FISH, debt, which may in many cases be unavoidable, is the least capable of dismantling Poverty, Inc.—because it often *is* Poverty, Inc.

Grants and Subsidies

Successful FISHers are always on the hunt for grants from governmental and philanthropic sources because these funds do not have to be repaid. These sources generally seek no financial return, but they do require that their funds have a positive and measurable community impact. In the past few years, a tsunami of grant funds has descended on underinvested communities, but keep some cautions in mind. First, in general, these pools of money are leveling off or even shrinking. In the 1980s, a developer creating new affordable housing could assume that federal grant sources would provide 20 percent of the capital needed. This has been decreasing steadily regardless of which political party controls the budget. Today, those sources provide only 6 percent of the needed capital.

There has also been decline at the state level. Most states face a day of reckoning as unfunded pension commitments become due. In Oregon, municipalities everywhere are cutting programs in order to pay faster into the retirement system.

Another word of caution about government grants: Sadly, many governmental programs actually harm the communities that they were designed to improve. It is important to minimize the role of government in a vulnerable community, because that limits the harm caused by corruption and discrimination.

A growing trend in grant making is community-based decision-making for government grant awards. While it is a step in the right direction, there is a reality here that surprised me when I experienced it directly. Studies and my experience show that the more unequal the community, the less effective community-based government grants are in targeting the poor.

A third word of caution is that federal funding is almost all siloed. The bureaucrats who write the rules are so narrow in their understanding of the problem to be solved that they end up creating grant programs that harm people rather than help. Knowing this, responsible social service agencies go to the large philanthropies who understand this dynamic; there, they solicit the funds that they need to layer onto the federal grant so that the program actually becomes helpful.

A form of grants from the federal government that has a more positive impact are tax credits. To the developer, the business, the individual, or the nonprofit that benefits from them, they function like a grant in that they never have to be repaid. But unlike federal grant programs, they come with a lot fewer program-related strings attached. At their core, tax credits are much more free-market oriented than program grants are. About $3.5 billion of new markets tax credits are available per year for use in low-income neighborhoods. Low-income housing tax credits, which cost the federal government about $6 billion per year, finance about 90 percent of all of the affordable housing units in the US. A challenge for groups that want to leverage tax credits is that the pie is fixed, and if a new group wants a piece, everyone else's piece will necessarily be smaller. The entrenched interests are well able to defend their turfs.

The last category for sources of grants is foundations. We are living in the golden age of philanthropy, and US-based foundations are sitting on more than one trillion dollars in assets. Internationally, the foundations like to run their own programs, but in the US they like to give money to others to run programs. In North America, the categories that foundations give to, in order of dollars gifted, are education, health, human services/social welfare, arts and culture, and nonprofits. Getting grants from philanthropic sources that actually help the community long-term is desirable because, like the decision-makers at CDFIs, grant-makers are frequently holistic and mission-driven. A big growth area for most US foundations is program-related investments, which is a management strategy whereby the foundation participates in community building projects as a debt or equity investor *in addition to* as a grantor.

Bonds

FISHers may find that their community-building project can be financed by a bond. Here in Oregon, the state makes it pretty easy to navigate the legal and regulatory framework, and institutional investors will buy bonds. If my charter school project had not been stopped by the local school board, we would have financed the $8 million building with a bond. It would have been better than bank debt because we would be in direct communication with the bondholders, many of whom are supportive of charter schools, and there would have been no bank in the middle with its own agenda.

Social impact bonds are slowly getting off the ground in the US and hold great promise for changing the social services sector by introducing pay-for-success incentives. The idea behind those incentives is to get government out of the services business by working to define desired outcomes and payment rates. Then the nonprofit issues a social impact bond and uses the proceeds to launch the service. When the desired outcome is achieved, government pays the nonprofit, who pays off the bondholders with interest and keeps a little net profit for their troubles. Social impact bonds are such a serious threat to Poverty, Inc. that our government is going to have to study them for a long time before they are widely adopted. A very, very long time.

Equity Investments

An equity investment puts cash into the community project or business and, in return, requires the owner of that project or business to share profits or increases in net asset value with the equity holder.

Equity is very attractive in an underinvested community because it puts the investor on the side of the community. If the project or business prospers, the investor prospers. If it fails, the investor loses. Private equity funds, high-net-worth individuals, and family offices are sources of equity in America's cities and in the poor communities right outside the city gates, but they may not be accessible at all in our overlooked rural places.

The new opportunity zone (OZ) tax regime is becoming a game-changing source of equity for urban, suburban, and rural neighborhoods. OZ offers ridiculous tax benefits for people who have unrealized capital gains. It is thought that over $6 trillion in assets are sitting on the sidelines in America because selling them to put them to use would trigger an onerous capital gain tax charge. When investors instead sell an asset and put that gain into one of America's OZs, they get relief from a lot of those taxes. Although it is early days for OZ, it is already the biggest neighborhood stimulus ever. Industry player JPAmerica estimates that over $100 billion has been invested in just the first three years of the program.

Equity investments can have a big impact with micro-entrepreneurs, small businesses, and emerging businesses in low-income communities. New business formation and growth is one of the most powerful activities that FISHers can encourage because the businesses create jobs, wealth, and social capital. At my Sunrise Center Kitchen, at any one time, about fifteen newbie businesspeople are busily creating a new future for themselves. Because most of these businesses are growing, they have growing pains that can be cured by cold hard cash. Some debt might be available per standard underwriting guidelines, but the entrepreneur who makes that choice risks catastrophe if he breaks the covenants. The missing piece is equity. These newbie businesspeople may not even know what equity is and how it functions, nor do they have the bonding social capital to raise money from friends and family, or the bridging social capital to go find an angel investor. So they fail to progress in their businesses. Equity is the glass ceiling for the entrepreneur in America's Rockwoods.

Our communities need equity investments from impact investors, whether individuals, family offices, corporations, or philanthropies. We need visionary, caring investors who are willing to cross barriers with their capital. The decision by a rich person to invest in a poor person is a radical statement of affinity with human flourishing.

But there are some challenges that come built-in when a high-net-worth investor chooses to engage in a poor community. Some of these challenges are structural, but the biggest ones are personal. Structurally, investors do not understand or even see these communities. Data is hard to come by. The entrepreneurs in the poor communities might not be sophisticated financially or even speak English very well. The high-net-worth investors fear deceptive financial appraisals, are concerned about how they will sell their stake, and want assets that they can go after if the owner refuses to repay. These objections and more are normal and valid for all equity investors.

> **The decision by a rich person to invest in a poor person is a radical statement of affinity with human flourishing.**

The solution is to put in place a mediating institution that brings to the table both the impact investor and the business and gets a cut of the action for doing so. We created our Oregon Community Capital subsidiary for this very purpose, with a special emphasis on raising and deploying opportunity zone dollars to emerging small businesses and to real estate projects. To the impact investor, we look and feel like any professionally managed private equity fund. And to the business owner or developer, we look and feel like a community-based organization that understands that place matters and that these business owners need more support than the average. Business support organizations are a big category in the US today. They already have people out in "the soup" who are engaging, coaching, and creating grassroots businesses. They know how to minimize risk in culturally specific ways and create a double bottom line result: profits and community benefit.

As I work with new impact investors, I see that they are challenged on a personal level in ways that really surprise them. Many have created investable capital because they trade and speculate in stocks. They see their money world on a screen, and that screen is far removed from the real world of small business. For them, entering a broken community with risk capital means reducing their reliance on speculation and increasing their exposure to real results from real operating businesses. Newbie impact investors need an intermediary organization.

Not only do some impact investors not trust their own understanding of business fundamentals; some also really hate to enter personally into an equity investment. The really rich guys I know are also the loneliest, least purposeful people that I know. They've driven away everyone, they do not collaborate, and they will *not* let go of their assets. To save their own lives, they need to invest in communities and thereby enter personally into the story.

And that's the thing. Once someone has accumulated wealth, it's personal whether they want it to be or not. Just as when Renaldo knocked at my door ten years ago, a response is required. It is healing for both parties when the investor is willing to cross the divide. And if the investor isn't willing, then they are part of the problem. I wish that I had had an intermediary institution like our subsidiary Oregon Community Capital, Inc. when I decided to risk. I probably would have established a relationship with the intermediary group first. Remember "I do my compassion at the wholesale level, not the retail level"? I didn't want to bear the pain of the entrepreneur. And eventually, when I grew enough to have a relationship with the business owner, I could have done it with the intermediary organization never very far away. I admit it—I was an emotourist! But I ended up committing deeply to a low-intensity, long-term investing of my time, talent, and treasure.

FISHers will be adept at putting all four of the forms of financial capital (debt, equity, grants, and bonds) into their broken neighborhoods. A recent $79 million mixed-use, commercial/residential project in California was financed through a mix of 27 percent equity, 40 percent grants, and 33 percent debt. Half was private money, and half was public money. Each plays its part, and each comes with drawbacks. The skillful mixing of different capital sources can make previously impossible projects possible.

INTELLECTUAL CAPITAL

FISHers grow the intellectual capital of the communities that they are working with by putting to work the financial, governance, operational, and strategic tools available. Community development can be complex and sophisticated. If someone is willing to gather and apply the know-how of the business, urban planning, health care, education, and other sectors to the needs of the whole community, they might find solutions to previously intractable problems. But not a lot of people have the know-how to develop effective community-wide strategies for transformation. Our nation's best and brightest are either on the sidelines or don't live in low-income communities. But a lack of residency status doesn't disqualify anyone. If a FISHer is willing to submit to the wisdom of the neighbors, then I encourage that FISHer to be present, and even to lead.

Know-how is one part of intellectual capital. *Data* is another part. I developed my own qualitative and quantitative data sets using the Speaks! and Knocks processes because, before that, few were available. But ten years on, Big Data is delivering on its potential to illuminate even the darkest alleys of America's cities. Many web-based data mining and visualization platforms now make it easy to drill down to the smallest level of granularity, the census tract. The "Prosperity Now Scorecard"[9] is but one example of point-and-click analysis that in the past would have taken an army of analysts.

The combination of know-how and data form the essential building block of modern community development: evidence-based intervention. I am never bashful about letting the data speak for itself. My organization constantly looks for ways to document our community, and we publish our findings online in the Rockwood Identity Atlas. The data closely ties to the facilitated conversations to tell us what needs to be done in order to drive human flourishing.

SOCIAL CAPITAL

FISHers who are place-based, technically skillful, and data-driven know that financial and intellectual capital are types of "top down" intervention. Social and human capital are types of "bottom up" intervention. Both have to work together to transform a community holistically. Elements of social capital that can be increased are anchor institutions, bonding capital, bridging capital, faith communities, and aspirational statements.

Anchor Institutions

One of the exciting new pieces of social infrastructure in the US is the anchor institution. This is a place-based, nongovernmental organization (NGO) that has as its mission quarterbacking the FISH initiatives. When I was the CEO of the Philippines' fourth-largest NGO, I saw for myself what a good quarterback could do. My NGO created the network that provided support for business co-ops, loans, healthy families, investments, education, health care, spiritual growth, disaster relief, and environmental cleanup. Anchors have the skills of entrepreneurship: seeing opportunities, cutting through complexity, quickly innovating, using capital efficiently, and networking. They are there to turn one-off success into replicable and scalable strategies. Examples here in the US are David Doig's Chicago Neighborhood Initiatives, Local Initiatives Support Corporation, Harlem Children's Zones, Houston's BakerRipley, Codman Square Health Center, Cleveland's University Circle, University of Chicago, and my still-young CDCO. National anchor institutions work with local ones to achieve scale.

Anchors do things like set up a land trust, create public-private partnerships, serve as hubs or backbones for collective impact projects, run regional alternative food systems, advocate for legal or policy change, nurture social entrepreneurs, analyze data, build hub-and-spoke systems to distribute resources to smaller organizations, syndicate capital for regional projects, and build bridges across unrelated segments of the systems. They are a new thread in the larger fabric that shares the load with government. Funding for anchors is frequently an ad-hoc affair, and we need better and more stable funding sources. Anchors are backed up by technical support from organizations like the Federal Reserve, the Urban Land Institute, the Rockefeller Foundation, the Christian Community Development Association, and many others.

Bonding and Bridging Capital

Anchor institutions understand that when social capital is raised along with human capital, communities discover their own narratives and move toward them. They help build bonding capital by running community centers like the Sunrise Center; they host community engagement at industrial scale, like the more than two thousand adults we have had in facilitated conversations; they incubate social entrepreneurs, like the ten new nonprofits that we have either started directly or helped along; they create and nurture affinity groups, like our forty-three-member Shalom Church Network, or the Rockwood Food System Collaborative; they stimulate cultural expression, as we do twice a year with our cultural festivals; they identify gaps and invite others to fill them, as we did with new affordable housing; and they keep the community's agenda on track, as we are doing in our advocacy work. Anchors also build bridging capital by hosting regional convenings, as we did when we hosted the first public-office candidate forum that Rockwood had ever seen; they communicate the aggregate needs of the community outward, as we have done with Oregon's governor; they engage outside experts and technical support, as we have done with the USDA and the Federal Reserve; they advertise opportunities to financial capital sources; they collect and report data, as we did with Rockwood Knocks's tens of thousands of data points; they set up navigation relationships between experts and neighbors; and they gatekeep (in a good way) when army-builders want to hijack the community's agenda.

The anchor institutions—no matter how small or how large, no matter how widely or narrowly they are recognized as legitimate players, and no matter the size of the budget—never leave the table. They are all about fidelity to the process, to being a neutral player full of goodwill and taking a broad view, and to taking on the system that certainly does not want the anchor institution to anchor anything.

Faith Communities

Anchor institutions recognize that faith communities of all stripes are essential players in community transformation. To the anchor institution, it may not really matter which faith is dominant in a community, because all churches, mosques, and temples have in common a permanent commitment to place. It may require many patient invitations before churches, mosques, or temples respond, however. Some have no interest in supporting their people in being outward focused, and some don't even have a theology that suggests they should. Others believe that they must drive the agenda for the whole community. I have worked patiently with my own faith community. In the past four years, especially, I have seen a huge swing outward. But not all megachurches have responded like mine. One of the megachurches that sits just outside Rockwood pledged a much-needed $25,000 per year for three years, brought me up on stage to make the pitch to donors, and then promptly "forgot" all about writing the check. I have found that at least one of the four core values (Reconciliation, It's Personal, Build Bridges Not Armies, and Never Leave the Table) at some point breaks against the internal dysfunction of every faith community. Still, they usually have a desire to become more relevant to the poor, so eventually most come around. When they do, amazing resources can get unleashed.

Aspiration

Anchor institutions lead the community into aspirational conversations about where the community wants to go. We convene disconnected organizations and talk about common visions. We ask them to tell us what they are willing to risk in order to see the vision accomplished, what assets they are willing to bring, and what liabilities they are struggling with. My first attempt to develop a regional plan got off to a good start. We tabled it, however, until wealthy philanthropies were ready to make commitments to fund this work.

We are still waiting.

It's important when I am doing bridging work of this kind that I insist that outside assets actually pay to enter into the internal discussion. We can only get so far for free. I have to get the emotourists to stop extracting from my community so that they can feel better about their work.

HUMAN CAPITAL

Finally, FISHers work to build human capital. I have talked about human capital extensively in this book. Everyone knows about "infrastructure" items like roads, buildings, and other elements of the built environment. But there are health and food infrastructures. Education, jobs, business support, and social services can all be worked on as infrastructure plays too. The human capital that these systems build (or extract) usually have little to do with the government and everything to do with the free market. Sometimes they deliver value and sometimes they do not. But *all* of them that are open-minded and full of goodwill benefit when FISHers come alongside of them to help them succeed.

Teaching our communities to FISH means making available the financial, intellectual, social, and human capital required to get the job done. Over time, communities will use this capital to build their own versions of human flourishing. It is a beautiful thing when a community begins to heal itself.

America is at a crossroads.

America is at a crossroads. Down one road lies the systemic structure that used to serve us well but has now become toxic. Poveteers run the gigantic bureaucratic machine for the creation and maintenance of hopelessness. They build and maintain the wall against which possibilities crash. To preserve themselves, these systems *must* ensure that new social movements and new anchor institutions fail to generate new futures. They must not let us win—or even appear viable.

Down the other road is a new systemic infrastructure that opens new possibilities. It is place-based and market driven. It harnesses financial, intellectual, social, and human capital for the benefit of all. Development activities lead and inform betterment activities, which eventually reduce the need for relief activities.

Under the Hood: Notes on How We Set and Run the Businesses

*T*he Community Development Corporation of Oregon (CDCO) is pretty complicated. We have big-company acronyms and accounting policies and structure—which is weird to people who live in Rockwood because they see a homey, grassroots group. But we feel that we need that more formal structure if we are to achieve our goal of community transformation. Our 2021 operating budget was $10,000,000, which places us in the top 5 percent of all nonprofits nationwide. So when you look "under the hood," you see a corporation and not a mom-and-pop operation. Here are some notes on how and why we have put together our organization in the way that we have. I hope that it helps people in other communities imagine how they could get started.

FORMS OF INCORPORATION

Within our corporate structure, the CDCO has both for-profit and nonprofit corporations. Like a carpenter who has different tools in her tool belt for different jobs, I wanted both forms of incorporation available to me. Because I had an MBA and had already run both types of companies, I was comfortable with the complexity of this setup. I registered the CDCO as a nonprofit and applied for tax-exempt status from the IRS. Today the CDCO has a wholly owned for-profit subsidiary, Oregon Community Capital Inc., and two nonprofit subsidiaries: East County Housing and Oregon Capital Access Network. While all of this sounded daunting at the beginning, I knew that the main objective was to not limit what could be done in future years by limiting the legal and financial structure of the companies right from the get-go.

So why a community development corporation? A CDC is simply a nonprofit that is tax-exempt and that can access some federal funds that other tax-exempt nonprofits cannot. There might be around five thousand CDCs in the US, but nobody really knows. To form a CDC, you don't really need anyone's permission. There is no form to fill out or certification from the government. You just declare yourself to be one. You put it in your founding documents and reference it in your application to the IRS. No one ever checks up on you, and there are no standards to be met. In fact, if later you decide to stop acting like one, you just stop. So being a CDC in my mind meant that I could be extremely broad and flexible, and that there were no limitations. All upside, and no downside.

LITTLE, BIG, CORE, OR COLLABORATIVE?

Core to our strategy is the idea that we want to be perceived as little when we are working with our neighbors, and big when it matters to major philanthropies, investors, or governmental units. You can see what this looks like for yourself online. The CDCO's website (www. cdcoregon.org) looks like the $10 million organization that we are, but the websites of our subtending brands, say the Rockwood Food System Collaborative (www.rockwoodfsc.org), may look a little more homespun. Our brands that are "of the community" intentionally invite engagement. An example is the Sunrise Center site (www.sunrise-center.cpm), which invites our neighbors to envision themselves and their narrative being experienced there. The Oregon Community Capital, Inc. site (www.oregoncap.com) looks and feels to investors like a private equity firm. The East County Community Health site (www.ecchealth.org) signals that it is part of the health care system.

Another piece of our strategy is to put all of our brands on a path out of the nest. Remember that our goal is to build the social capital of the area, not to run social services. We want these brands to become their own worlds of volunteers, fundraising, governance, and strategies. We've already let the Shalom Rockwood Network of churches become its own freestanding network, and it has worked out great. You can see this strategy on the website for East County Community Health (www.ecchealth.org), which will hardly have to change when this business unit becomes freestanding.

MANAGEMENT PRACTICES

Our rapid growth, along with our holistic approach, has made managing this nonprofit a very complex task. Especially in America, nonprofits have needed to professionalize in response to government regulation and philanthropic expectations. Today's nonprofits are much more complex to manage than most similarly sized for-profit companies, and yet the wage rates for skilled nonprofit executives are lower. I had to invent methodologies for managing networks of people on a shoestring, using volunteers, and it took me a long time to figure it all out. A big piece of the puzzle fell into place when we learned that almost all of the software that we needed was available for free or at a deeply reduced cost from the big names like Microsoft, Salesforce, and QuickBooks. Setting all of these systems up is a mind-numbing chore, of course, but we were always able to find volunteers who were handy with a mouse. Salesforce is just one of the customer-relationship management (CRM) platforms out there, and it may not always be the best one, but it is free to nonprofits. It has so many options—maybe too many—that we had to have it set up for our way of running community processes. We found a young programmer eager to demonstrate his skills on the platform so that he could launch his own consulting practice, and we were a great first reference account. Having this tool at the heart of our operation has proven to be powerful. Because we have a record of all of the events, campaigns, and interests of now eleven thousand people, plus a record of how they are related to others in the database, we often see connections that others do not. I had a bank board member chide me once because I had not considered her branch for a loan. "You didn't even call us," she complained. She didn't know that even as she was venting, I was looking up the branch in our database and found that, yes, indeed one of my team members reached out to the manager on a particular date and got no response back. "Oh," she said. "Would you send that to me in writing?" Yes, indeed.

I also had to set up human resources systems to support my robust volunteer culture and to comport with Oregon's overbearing labor laws. I wanted to overcome the natural tendency of volunteers to float in and out by treating them like highly valued employees. I wanted them to know that their activities, far from being just extras, are mission-critical. I have many employee and volunteer classifications: salaried non-exempt, hourly exempt, consultant or contractor, volunteer who is paid by a partner organization, staff volunteer, and volunteer (all depending on whether they have job descriptions, have a supervisor or supervise others, and have performance metrics). People in staff volunteer or volunteer positions sign all of the same policies[10] as any of the other classifications, as appropriate for their role. Just because a member of staff is a volunteer does not mean that she cannot supervise a paid employee or contractor.

One of the classifications covers our volunteers who are paid by a partner organization. I was surprised when another organization wanted to "give" us a worker, but it has happened several times. For example, a local nonprofit that supplements the education at a local school had an employee who was tasked with community-building activities, and her valuable work did not really fit with the rest of the nonprofit's educational programs. Recognizing that Tiffany fit better at the CDC, they continued to pay her but had her work for me. Another organization called One Collective "gave" us one full-time and two part-time staffers for our first few years. These arrangements were covered by memoranda of understanding and functioned more like an easy partnership than a strict reporting relationship. These volunteers to us, employees to them, are so highly qualified that I would never be able to afford them.

ACCOUNTING POLICIES AND PROCEDURES

Since our start, we have been writing and compiling an accounting policies and procedures manual, because we expected that someday we would be big. Version 1.0 was three pages—humble, but a start. As our businesses flourished and complexity increased, we added more to it and called it version 1.1. Eight years later, we are finally big enough to require an audit of our books, and our version 3.1 document is robust and complete.

To accomplish our goals, our accounting, management, and reporting practices must be excellent because the governmental units and major philanthropies demand it. In general, the complex requirements from many of these funding sources have gotten out of hand. One grant request that we recently released to a foundation required seventeen separate documents.

A common complaint that I hear from leaders in Oregon is that all of this has become too complex. "We *could* go for these grants, but it's just too complicated," goes the refrain. Yes, it is complicated. Yes, some of the federal forms (we're looking at you, FEMA) are brain damaging. But the money is big and it is free. If our underinvested communities are to receive the proper amount of investment, then somebody has to bear the pain of navigating the bureaucracy's complexity. And that somebody, at least in our corner of the state, is the CDCO.

MISSION, VISION, CORE VALUES, TAGLINE

Holding together a large and complicated organization requires us to constantly revisit our mission, vision, core values, and tagline. Hardly a meeting goes by in which one of the leaders does not read aloud one or more of these documents.

Our tagline is, "Working with our neighbors to make Rockwood a place where everyone can learn, earn and belong."

Our Vision is:

We dream of communities:
      with rising levels of prosperity;
      where employment and decent housing are
         accessible by all;
      where health outcomes are excellent;

where vibrant community life emerges
   from diversity; and
where all show compassion to those in need.

Our Mission is:
   We provide pathways for moving from
      poverty to prosperity by:
   Expanding the supply of decent housing;
   Supporting economic development;
   Increasing access to health care and
      encouraging healthy behavior;
   Creating and sustaining public-private partnerships;
   Aligning the strategies and resources of the educa-
      tional, faith-based, governmental, capital, social
      service, business, and health care sectors.

Our Core Values are:

Our Four Core Values	
It's Personal	Everyone that works with us and for us is personally involved in the lives of our community. This keeps us relationally connected to our neighbors and community. We intentionally invest in relationships as we invest in other aspects of community development.
Build Bridges, Not Armies	Everything we do is built on an ethic of inclusion, diversity, and justice. Reconciliation is hard work and we are committed to building diverse relational bridges that lead to true justice.

Reconciliation	We pursue the disconnected and bring them into relationship through what is often hard relational work that is rooted in listening, humility, and learning.
Never Leave the Table	We are here for the long-term, even when things get hard. We do not launch programs and then leave, but we are here till our vision has been accomplished.

Resources for Learning More

*H*ans Rosling writes the best stuff about how to understand the data around income and poverty. His website www.gapminder.com is up-to-date, and his book *Factfulness* (New York: Flatiron Books, 2018) is a quick and funny read.

Poverty, Inc. is a documentary and accompanying website that introduces the world of poverty alleviation. It sometimes paints with too broad a brush, but it is still a reasonably informative and entertaining ninety minutes.

When Helping Hurts: How to Alleviate Poverty Without Hurting the Poor...and Yourself by Brian Fikkert and Steve Corbett (Chicago:

Moody Publishers, 2014) is a thoughtful critique of Poverty, Inc. You will see that many of its themes are echoed in this book.

Our Last Option by Andrew Marin (Denver: Patheos Press, 2015)—only available as an ebook—is a much better overview of building community than books that are twice its size.

Community: The Structure of Belonging by Peter Block (Oakland, CA: Berrett-Koehler Publishers, 2018) is a classic and foundational book that continues to inform and challenge the work of building community.

The Second Mountain by David Brooks (New York: Random House, 2020) traces the author's personal commitment to rebuilding community, and explains how these communities will save America.

Debt: The First Five Thousand Years by David Graeber (Brooklyn: Melville House, 2014) is long and fascinating. If you weren't convinced that debt is the last resort for building wealth in a community before, you will be after.

Investing in What Works for America's Communities: Essays on People, Place & Purpose by the Federal Reserve Bank of San Francisco and the Low Income Investment Fund, and *What It's Worth: Strengthening the Financial Future of Families, Communities and the Nation* by the Federal Reserve Bank of San Francisco and the Corporation for Enterprise Development, are a series of essays that every FISHer should read. You can get them both for free from the Fed.

Confronting Suburban Poverty in America by Elizabeth Kneebone and Alan Berube (Washington, DC: Brookings Institution Press, 2014) showed me that every city has a Rockwood.

Acknowledgments

Ten years ago, Kiesel said, "When you look back at this, you are going to say two opposite things about it. They are going to both be true. The first is, 'This did not happen because of me,' and the second is, 'None of this would have happened if it weren't for me.'" The way I have chosen to write this story is with myself at the center of it, which necessarily diminishes the role of others. I wanted readers to know what it feels like, what it looks like, what it sounds like, to enter into a distressed community and to help it open up new possibilities, in the hope that it will help readers find the courage to act. This writerly decision meant that in many places, where I say *I*, I really mean *we*. I never took credit for the work of someone else, but I also needed to move on with the story by keeping the list of characters short.

The "we's" who have hung in the longest and given the most are my wife, Lynn Ketch, Scott and Vicki McCracken, Vanessa and

Willie Chambers, Scott and Vicki Gillis, Jason and Nikki Albelo, Bill and Kathy Kieselhorst, Ron Graves, and Elaine and Mike Edrington.

The "we's" who have had a positive impact for a season or for a specific aspect of our work are Pam Ferguson, Loren Sickles, Christine Sanders, Josh Fuhrer, Patrik McDade, Eugene Wallace, Carl Talton, Hai Nguyen, Michael Jacobsen, Paul and Kim Young, and Stephen and Molly Ketch.

Thank you to my Guides (plus those named above) who brought me to a better place of understanding: Dr. Peter Clark, David Doig, and David Austin.

The late Kit Shields coined the term *poveteers*.

The Flourishing Community
www.flourishing community.com

Brad Ketch and his associates are available to begin the conversation about how to bring hope to your distressed places. We invite you to visit www.flourishingcommunity.com for more information.

Notes

1 Elizabeth Kneebone and Alan Berube, *Confronting Suburban Poverty in America* (Washington, DC: Brookings Institution Press, 2014).

2 David Brooks, *The Second Mountain* (New York: Random House, 2020).

3 Peter Block, *Community* (Oakland, CA: Berrett-Koehler, 2008).

4 Michelle Alexander, *The New Jim Crow* (New York: The New Press, 2020).

5 Bryan Stevenson, *Just Mercy* (New York: One World, 2014).

6 Alan Mallach, *The Divided City: Poverty and Prosperity in Urban America* (Washington, DC: Island Press, 2018). This book does a good job of dispelling the myths about poverty.

7 Quentin Brummet. *The Effects of Gentrification on the Well-Being and Opportunity of Original Resident Adults and Children.* Federal Reserve Bank of Philadelphia, July 2019, 19–30; *Does Gentrification Displace Poor Children?* New Evidence from New York City Medicaid Data. National Bureau of Economic Research, May 2019.

8 David Graeber, *Debt: The First 5,000 Years* (Brooklyn: Melville House, 2014).

9 https://scorecard.prosperitynow.org/

10 Accounting Policies and Procedures, Background Check, Computer and Internet Use, Confidentiality, Conflict of Interest, Debit Card Use, Drug and Alcohol Policy, Employee Handbook, Guidelines for Volunteers Who Transport Residents, Parental Waiver for Child to Participate in Our Activities, Personal Auto Use Reimbursement, Policy on Community Navigators, Sexual Harassment Policy, Sunrise Center Key and Passcode Policy, Tenant Rights and Responsibilities, Volunteer Driver Checklist, and Whistleblower Procedure.